T0034830

SEEING GOD in the
Sweet Ordinary

BECKY STRAHLE

HARVEST HOUSE PUBLISHERS
EUGENE, OREGON

CONTENTS

Seeing God in the Sweet Ordinary of Your Story...5

Be Still..15

Do Not Be Afraid..................................21

Masterpiece.......................................27

The Faithful List.................................33

Tumbled Hearts....................................39

Tending to Our Garden 45

The Beauty of Change.............................51

Rest Easy...59

Joy Comes...65

The Great Gathering...............................71

The Thorn...77

Salt + Light......................................83

Journey to Restoration 89

Diving into New Territory.........................95

Sweet Surrender..................................101

High Hopes.......................................107

The Scent of Worship.............................115

Change Your Focus................................121

Paint the Vision.................................127

'Tis So Sweet to Trust in Jesus.................133

Perfect Peace....................................139

God with Us......................................145

Safe Place.......................................151

The Gift of Blessing.............................157

Listen for His Voice.............................163

Walk Worthy......................................169

Seeing God in the Sweet Ordinary of Your Story

Finally, brothers and sisters, whatever is true, whatever is noble, whatever is right, whatever is pure, whatever is lovely, whatever is admirable—if anything is excellent or praiseworthy—think about such things.

PHILIPPIANS 4:8

Hi, friend! I'm so honored you're here. And I'm grateful for this opportunity to walk with you as we learn to see God in our daily moments and in the bigger twists and turns of life's path.

Is there a part of your story that is difficult, and yet it is also the very thing that leads you to lean into God's embrace? Maybe grief has overshadowed your heart for a long time, or a spirit of fear has taken control. I've experienced those things. And I'm thankful because the lessons I've learned have increased my faith and given me a heart for encouraging others.

When we are aware of our wounds, worries, and "what next?" moments and surrender them to God, they can usher us into His strength and promises. But when we are distracted, our concerns and the lies we believe can lead us inward, and we can easily miss

God's presence in our sweet, ordinary days.

In 2009, I was a young mama struggling with depression, living in the bitter cold of Minnesota. To get me back on track, the Lord graciously brought my attention to blogging. I had no idea the lifeline that this simple act of obedience would become. It turned my focus away from in-the-moment misery, and I started looking for the good in everyday things. God began showing me His fingerprints on my life. I snapped pictures of nature, our two daughters, our home, my husband. Ordinary things that I had begun to take for granted became huge revelations of God's goodness and provision. I hadn't written consistently before, but God's story began pouring out of me. Everything was tied to Him. I suddenly felt as if I'd been given the sweetest gift—a glimpse into the secret world of supernatural gratitude.

Eventually, I started a business designing faith-based jewelry for women. I called it Farmgirl Paints, and over time, it grew and became successful. It became my identity in a way. What a dream job! I hand-stamped encouraging words on beautiful leather cuffs. Yet they were other people's words. And while it was wonderful for a season, I began to sense that God had something even more personal and purposeful for me to do.

In 2018 I felt led to lay down my business and go a different direction. I knew I was supposed to get back to my giftings—my love of painting and writing—but I didn't know what that meant. After months of waiting, the Lord "downloaded" the new plan. I could barely write down the ideas fast enough, but eventually, the next steps became clear. I would write monthly letters to my community and begin painting again. The words "Tell them they are loved" rolled around in my mind. So with a little trepidation, I started writing love letters. Devotions of encouragement flowed out of me.

Reminders that Jesus is the source of our purpose, happiness, and our salvation.

God warned me this new direction would require patience. Not everyone would understand. But despite those concerns, I set off in obedience . . . and He was right! It was a slow build, but each month I could feel His presence. My dependence on Him for creativity tethered me to His heart with intimacy and trust. That's a good place to be.

After several months of going in this new direction, I started to feel a bit low-energy and aimless. Old habits of negative thinking began to reappear. I felt the Holy Spirit urging me to visit an online friend and fellow artist in Beaufort, South Carolina. Making that trip required a lot of trust, but within minutes of meeting Melissa, those old negative mindsets began to break away, and I became acutely aware of the words I had been telling myself. Words have enormous power, and mine were setting limitations and instilling fear instead of faith.

That trip was pivotal in freeing me to pursue my art. I started painting BIG! I got out of my head and started having fun, and with every swipe of my paintbrush, I could feel the Holy Spirit taking the lead. I was no longer the artist—He was! I had a beautiful greenhouse studio on my property, with wide-open doors and praise music filling the air. I've never been trained in the arts, so the awe I felt in the holy hush after finishing each painting left me in tears. I would stand back with paint-splattered hands and a tear-stained face and weep because I knew the art was sacred. It was 100 percent God-inspired.

What words do you hear, speak, or believe that tear down your spirit? What cycles of worry devour your hope? Those, my friend,

are not from the Lord. You will know when words and nudges are from Him because He ushers in peace. Philippians 4:6-7 says, "Do not be anxious about anything, but in every situation, by prayer and petition, with thanksgiving [that's a prayer how-to right there], present your requests to God. And the peace of God, which transcends all understanding, will guard your hearts and your mind in Christ Jesus."

Fill your mind with the reassurance of your faith. Remind yourself of the truths of who you are. *My God is for me, not against me* (Romans 8:31). *Greater is He who is in me than he who is in the world* (1 John 4:4). *I'm a new creation in Christ Jesus; old things are passed away, and all things are becoming new* (2 Corinthians 5:17).

Maybe you've heard these Scriptures over the years, but they've lost their meaning . . . or maybe the authority of those words didn't sink in. Don't ever forget—these are *fighting words*. Speaking God's Word from your lips is truth and power. Even when our hearts are racing and fear is crippling us, our faith increases and our strength rebounds when we quote Scripture!

Some months I wrestle to create the love letters and art, but I still have peace because I know it's God's work. I speak His promises instead of my fear. This book is a compilation of those love letters inspired by daily encounters with the Lord and the God-breathed art I am blessed to create. I didn't set out to write a book, but He brought me to it. The fact that it's in your hands is another confirmation that no matter how ordinary or insignificant we might feel, God, the Maker of the universe, has a plan in place.

As you read each page and take in every image, ask the Holy Spirit to reveal Himself to you. When I share little pieces of my life, think on the ways God is shaping and strengthening your story. We all have experiences that connect us to Him. He is the Author of our faith, and hearing someone's testimony can help us on our own journey with Him.

The ordinary is truly spectacular when you look at life through the lens of grace and witness God's presence everywhere. All that we've been given, all that we hold dear—every heartbreaking experience, every cry of despair, every burst of joy and feeling of triumph—ties us to our Maker and intricately sets us apart for His glory.

You are so very loved, my friend.
May every page, every image, help you
think on and live from this great truth.

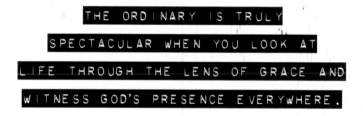

Be Still

Be still, and know that I am God; I will
be exalted among the nations, I will be
exalted in the earth.

PSALM 46:10

Have you ever sensed God nudging you to be still and get ready for change?

For me, it started as a nagging feeling in the back of my mind. I couldn't make out the words, but I knew things were shifting. Burnout in my work had set in. What used to be exciting and inspiring felt contrived and forced. I heard a whisper: *Let your helpers go.*

I dug in my heels and responded, *Not yet, Lord.*

Then the whisper became urgent. God was clearly asking me to let go of the business I had created. The day had come to do something different, and fear rose in my heart. The grief of laying down my business, my "baby," was real. I felt like I had a neon sign over my head that flashed "dead man walking." Who was I if I wasn't this business? I had crossed over from knowing my calling without doubt to flailing without purpose.

Vision gives me a reason to wake up in the morning. Without it, I don't know what to do with myself. And yet when He led me to lay it down, I trusted that something else would take its place—not knowing that the waiting would make me feel crazy. Then silly. Then the feelings stopped altogether. A quiet came. I waited months for God to reveal next steps.

Maybe that's where you are right now—in a place of waiting and quiet obedience. No one is noticing. The reaping hasn't begun yet, but the seeds have been planted. You are in complete darkness, waiting for His work to show, waiting for the beauty to burst through.

Finally, the "download" came with little tidbits of a dream emerging. *There will be phases. It will look something like this. Tell them they are loved.* The words "love letters" tumbled around in my mind. I knew I would be sharing God's hope. My curiosity was met with His whisperings to my spirit: *It will be a slow build.*

As it turned out, "slow build" was code for this: *You will do it without applause or affirmation. You will do it even when no one seems to get it. You will follow through when you are a little scared and it seems like there* 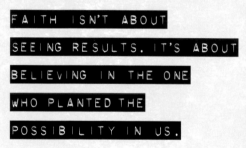 *is no point. You will push when you want to fold. You will question everything and struggle with doubt. The only thing that will keep you going is the hushed reminder . . . it will be a slow build. Do it because I am bringing you into something new. Don't chase the old. Don't look back. Don't try to figure it out. I will build this vision. When you feel like you are in a dark place . . . hold on to My Word. The day is coming when the darkness will turn to light, when the struggle will become fulfilled promises. Do it because I am your God.*

It's challenging when we don't see the progress we long for. Maybe we've even moved backward! But faith isn't about seeing results. It's about believing in the One who planted the possibility in us. It's about trusting the One who created us from nothing and has big plans for our lives. Faith is walking out that plan by holding on to every morsel deposited and waiting for it to "become."

Through the stillness, God invites us to stop trying to figure everything out so we can acknowledge who He is. And who is He? He's the Creator of everything. He is our defender, our safe place, our biggest fan. We don't have to worry, strive, or fear, because He's got us.

No matter what we are going through here on earth, darkness is nothing compared to the light. When it's time to move into His plans for you, He'll give you what you need to do just that.

"After waiting patiently, Abraham received what was promised" (Hebrews 6:15). Yes! God did not forget His promises to His people through the ages, and He will not forget His promises to me and to you.

God's next step for you is coming, my friend. And the beauty and light that emerge on the landscape of your life will be worth the wait.

You Are So Loved

The Lord will fight for you;
you need only to be still.

EXODUS 14:14

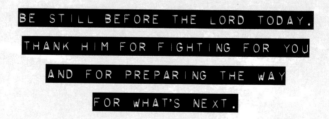

BE STILL BEFORE THE LORD TODAY.
THANK HIM FOR FIGHTING FOR YOU
AND FOR PREPARING THE WAY
FOR WHAT'S NEXT.

Thank You, Lord, for loving me and seeing what I walk through on a daily basis. When my mind is quiet, I know You have me in a place of restoration and submission.

Fill my days with Your divine purpose. Fill my sails with Your wind and direction. I trust in You completely because Your Word is a lamp for my feet and a light on my path. As it guides me, it reminds me that You have a plan in place.

Help me to remember that faith isn't about results but is about relationship with You. When I wait and watch for Your movement in my life, I am being faithful. I vow not to forget Your promises, believing that You hold me dear.
In Jesus's name, amen.

Do Not Be Afraid

The angel of the Lord encamps around those who fear him, and he delivers them.

PSALM 34:7

A few years back, my husband and I bought a house—sight unseen! We were giddy with excitement and felt the potential for disappointment was worth it. Even though we had never done anything this risky or renovated a home before, we felt God's leading.

Before long, that sense of possibility started to fade. At every turn we were pushed to our limits. It stretched our marriage. It burdened us financially, physically, emotionally, and spiritually. It's hard to write this, but we were disappointed. Disappointed that we may have made a mistake. Disappointed that God may have allowed us to misstep. Have you ever had hard conversations in prayer about things not going as planned?

Why would He allow us to get in over our heads? Why wasn't this easier? Fear was a constant battle. Even after the renovations were over, I struggled with an uneasiness that wouldn't lift. We prayed over the land and house. We walked it. We anointed the windows and doors. We poured oil up and down the lane and wrote Scriptures all over the floors and walls. We declared the property ours, but that feeling of ownership didn't come for a very long time. I battled fear daily. I wore it like a heavy yoke. I felt alone. Images of what it used to be, who lived there, and the exorbitant cost and sacrifice tormented my mind and at times filled me with dread and doubt.

I knew God wanted us to move forward, to take the land and make it an offering to Him without fear or hesitation. Yet even knowing that didn't change my heart right away.

It wasn't until God gave me a mental picture of the field in front of our house filled with angels that I felt like I wasn't alone anymore. This vision was so impactful, I knew I had to paint it. This was His land, and His angel army was in  position, ready to fight for us. Nothing was going to happen to us here! When anxiety threatened to steal my peace, remembering this image reminded me of His promise. My hope today is that this image and these words will also restore your peace and faith in God's promises for your journey.

The Lord knew fear would be our greatest challenge . . . which is why His Word repeats over and over the command and encouragement, "Fear not" and "Do not be afraid." In our human capacity, we sometimes stumble. We don't know the future. Our minds default to fear as a safety mechanism until we learn to lean into God's strength and provision.

Do you struggle with fear? Does it keep you from meeting new people? Learning new skills? Does it nip at your heels and freeze you from living fully? Think about David, who wrote most of the book of Psalms. When he was hiding in a cave, running for his life, afraid to make a move because Saul was out to kill him, God gave him these words: "The angel of the LORD encamps around those who fear him, and he delivers him" (Psalm 34:7). God delivered David from his fears and used his life for good. He can and will do that for you too.

This land became our training ground on how to trust the Lord. Eventually we named our property Hesed Hill because *hesed* refers to God's steadfast, loyal love. It's the love that we don't deserve. The family kind of love . . . through thick and thin. The never-failing love. He would use this place to demonstrate His faithfulness to us time and time again. The battle between fear and faith had been won. The angel army is in place. The Lord resides here.

I want you to envision your own home surrounded by such love, your life held in the palm of His hand. Because it is! Psalm 139:4-5 says, "Before a word is on my tongue you, LORD, know it completely. You hem me in behind and before, and you lay your hand upon me." Write those truths in the secret places of your heart and revisit them often. Then watch how the Lord is blessing you with a new vision, a new hope, and a new way through the fear.

You Are So Loved

So do not fear, for I am with you; do not be dismayed, for I am your God. I will strengthen you and help you; I will uphold you with my righteous right hand.

ISAIAH 41:10

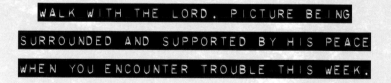

WALK WITH THE LORD. PICTURE BEING SURROUNDED AND SUPPORTED BY HIS PEACE WHEN YOU ENCOUNTER TROUBLE THIS WEEK.

Lord, thank You for surrounding me with Your presence, safety, and peace. No matter what I face, You are right by my side, and You equip me with the help I need to get through it. Lord, Your Word assures me over and over that I am not to be afraid. Forgive me when I go there.

Help me to rest in the promise that You have me in the palm of Your hand. You are for me and love me unconditionally. Break any stronghold of fear in me and set me free. I am more than a conqueror because of what You did for me on the cross and what You do in my life every day. I will not be afraid! In Jesus's name, amen.

Masterpiece

You created my inmost being; you knit me together in my mother's womb.

PSALM 139:13

Have you ever felt led to go outside your comfort zone? Maybe it was a call to obedience that made your stomach flutter and your heart race.

I did something brave—I took a trip with my daughter to France. Getting on a plane and traveling overseas without my husband was a new experience for me, and it made me extremely nervous. Regardless of my nerves, I knew I was supposed to go, so I prepped and planned and didn't give in to doubt. I think doing the unfamiliar challenges us in ways that safety never can. Pressing on, even when we're scared or anxious, can lead us to greater dependence on the One who made us and knows us best.

Yes, some of the what-ifs that swirled in my mind actually happened. Our luggage was lost. An army of ants invaded our bedroom. I had a physical ailment that challenged my pain tolerance all week. A taxi driver overcharged us because we didn't speak the language. But I didn't want those potential distractions to steal my joy and rob me of the present moment, so I resisted.

The reason we went was to attend an art retreat with real artists. I'll never forget the teacher coming by and giving little critiques. She spoke in artist lingo, assuming I understood. Having never attended art school, I didn't understand everything, but it didn't matter. She assumed I did, and I liked that feeling. The other students painted on large pieces of paper and canvas, while I found my safe, creative place on teeny tiny squares of Masonite.

I learned something about myself on that trip. Completion is my end game, and I need a clear starting place. I'm not a fan of the messy journey, and those big pieces of paper offered

EVERYTHING CHANGES WHEN WE TRULY GRASP THAT WE ARE HIS ART!

too much space and too much pressure to fill them with something worthy and wonderful. The expanse of nothing made me break into a cold sweat.

That annoying insecurity happens almost every time I start a new art project. I get struck with a flash of panic. The stark white canvas stares back at me taunting with endless possibilities and challenges. *Am I good enough to fill in this blank space? Can I create something beautiful?* These questions inevitably tempt me to doubt, but then I remember the faith it took to get on that plane. This little painting was my version of Claude Monet's *Chrysanthemums*. In Paris, at the Musée d'Orsay, I fell in love with this painting. His chunky strokes and wild floral abandon left me feeling inspired, and that's what art should do.

One of my favorite passages in the Bible is Psalm 139. The idea of my heavenly Father lovingly shaping you and me in our mothers' wombs, making me into me and you into you, is almost too much to fathom. When you face an intimidating moment—the equivalent of an international flight or a blank canvas in your own life—this imagery can fuel your bravery. You were intentionally made.

The Creator of all things personally shaped each of us before we were born. He purposed us into being. The blank canvas of your life or my life wasn't too much for Him. Each one of us is unique and spectacular. We are God's most intimate creations, and He took so much joy in knitting us together.

Everything changes when we truly grasp that we are His art! It takes the pressure off trying to be a perfect artist, mom, corporate CFO, or bakery chef because *we were created as masterpieces*. Our perfection is in our Creator. Our "art form" is our faith to try, to leap, to be the people God shaped us to become. We were formed and fashioned out of our heavenly Daddy's love for us, and we are here to serve a purpose. Does it get any better than that?

My friend, you can stand a little taller, reach a little further, and reflect His glory a little more every day in the way you bravely become you. Your life, relationships, home, family, and daily walk will shine brightly because of the One who created the one and only, beautiful you.

You Are So Loved

I praise you because I am fearfully and wonderfully made; your works are wonderful.

PSALM 139:14

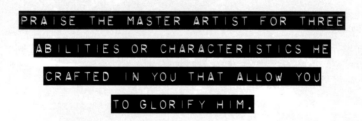

PRAISE THE MASTER ARTIST FOR THREE ABILITIES OR CHARACTERISTICS HE CRAFTED IN YOU THAT ALLOW YOU TO GLORIFY HIM.

Lord, I am grateful that even when I feel less than, You don't see me that way. I was created in Your image, and I was created to live out the plans You have for me. Help me see and appreciate the work that You did. The love and care that shaped me into being is still with me today as I navigate this life and its challenges.

Thank You for the gifts and talents You've imparted. Help me discover, trust, and use them for Your glory every day. Make me brave so I can step into new experiences to grow, stretch, and become all You've created me to be. I love You, Lord, because You first loved me even as You formed me in the very beginning. In Jesus's name, amen.

The Faithful List

**"I know the plans I have for you,"
declares the LORD, "plans to prosper
you and not to harm you, plans to give
you hope and a future."**

JEREMIAH 29:11

What does the phrase "God is faithful" mean to you? That question and your own answers are good things to have rolling around in your heart. To me it means a God who never fails. He sticks to His word. My thoughts land on the long list of God's attributes I have experienced over the years: steadfastness, dependability, trustworthiness, and so much more. These experiences, images, truths, and promises that He has impressed upon our hearts become what I call our faithful lists.

My faith-walk started when I asked Jesus into my heart as a little girl. My mama led me to Him at our kitchen table when I was six years old. After we prayed, I remember her taking my school picture, gluing it to a little white piece of paper, and writing John 3:16 on it. "God so loved the world, that he gave his only begotten Son, that whosoever believeth in him should not perish, but have everlasting life" (KJV). My faith was founded on that Scripture. His Word told me that because I believed in Jesus and what He did on the cross for me, I would spend eternity with Him. My mom said that the angels were rejoicing for me in heaven and that my name was being written in the Lamb's book of life. The idea of angels celebrating my decision from heaven stuck with me all these years, and it continues to assure my heart that I am loved and forgiven and that I have a promise of heaven.

Making that decision at such a young age has given me a lifetime of examples of His faithfulness to rest in and turn to when I need reminders and encouragement. This is where my faith has blossomed from religion into relationship. Dependency fosters relationship, and because of my history of intimate exchanges with the Lord, I have story after story of God meeting me in my hour of need. Faith is so much more than knowledge of who God is; it's experiencing His goodness in a tangible way. I know He loves me, because He's near. His presence is undeniable. Think of a time when you felt Him near. Did He carry you through a trial?

When I revisit my faithful list, I'm instantly taken back to a lifetime of answered *and* unanswered prayers. Yes! Even unanswered prayers have strengthened my trust in the Lord. Sometimes I prayed for something very specific, and it fell through. With the clarity of hindsight, I was able to look back and see God's merciful hand guiding me to something so much better. He knows! Can you recall a prayer that you thought wasn't fulfilled, yet the alternative outcome filled you with deep gratefulness? Perhaps that was a "blessing in disguise" moment.

I've learned over the years that the tighter I hold onto control with my prayers, the longer it seems I must wait for an answer. The key to praying is simply dying to self. First we say what we need or hope for or what we are giving over to God. Then—and this is the most important thing—we hold that want, hope, or offering loosely. This isn't always easy to do. But I have discovered there is a way to let go each time. We can release control by praying His will above our own.

On the inside I could be pleading for such and such to happen, yet my ultimate prayer is "Your will, not mine." Heaven forbid He should give me everything I've ever asked for! When I trust Him as my heavenly Daddy—the One 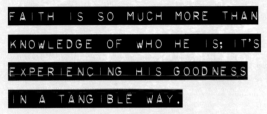 who knows the future and holds me in the palm of His hand—I have the assurance that no matter what, He has a plan for me and it's good. Because of God's steadfast loving-kindness, I have faith in the outcome!

The faithful list is what I run to when I'm uncertain of what's next. The faithful list is what I remember when my answer is taking too long. The faithful list is what comforts me when my world feels upside down. All I need to do is look back and count how many times He has taken care of me in the past.

His answer is coming. His timing, although painfully slow at times, is perfect. There is a plan in place, and He is always *good*. Now there is something to add to your faithful list!

You Are So Loved

We know that in all things God works for the good of those who love him, who have been called according to his purpose.

ROMANS 8:28

SO, FRIEND, WHAT WOULD BE ON YOUR FAITHFUL LIST? CREATE ONE TODAY. KEEP IT WHERE YOU WILL SEE IT AND CAN ADD TO IT DAILY.

Lord, thank You for having a big
picture in mind for me. Your Word
says that Your plan for me is good.
Help me trust in Your perfect will.
I know there will be hard times.
I've journeyed through many, and You
were with me. Our relationship has
allowed me to write my faithful list
and increase my faith. Your presence
assures and teaches me in the good
times and in the hard places.

You are good, faithful, and oh so
trustworthy! I will lay every concern
at Your feet and honor Your will
and Your best for me. Here I am
today with my prayer needs. I will
hold them loosely and trust in Your
response and Your ever-present mercy.
In Jesus's name, amen.

Tumbled Hearts

Jesus replied, "'Love the Lord your God with all your heart and with all your soul and with all your mind.' This is the first and greatest commandment. And the second is like it: 'Love your neighbor as yourself.'"

MATTHEW 22:37-39

One summer, our family visited a rock museum in Colorado. The shelves were lined with bowls of colorful, tumbled rocks that begged for my attention. One after another, the smooth stones found their way into my palm. My fingers stroked their refined, cool surfaces and each touch brought calm. The beautiful variations in color and line invited me to stop, look closer, and appreciate.

I wanted them all. Especially those shaped like hearts.

Later in the day, during a family hike, my gaze was drawn to rock after rock along the path. They weren't obvious treasures like the ones in the museum—they were the dusty, uninteresting rocks that few would interrupt their nature walk to look at. What if these rocks were the same kind I saw earlier in the shop? What if under that rough, bland exterior was a beautiful stone?

It didn't take long for my thoughts to follow a more personal trail. What if beneath my ordinary life and rough exterior was a hidden beauty? Maybe our lives need to be tumbled upside right and polished over and over until we are smooth and shiny. Imagine our imperfect selves being held in the Master's hand, His touch and care smoothing our edges and bumps until we can reflect His breathtaking mercy and glory.

Is there anything jagged in you that you can identify right now? Has grief, anger, or rejection formed crevices and scars? Have harsh words carved sharp edges?

Over the years, my experiences with hurt, rejection, and disappointment have shaken my belief that people are good. I've become a bit cynical. True confession: loving people can be challenging for me. I was lying in bed the other night thinking about the Lord and how He sees beyond the person. He sees the pain. He sees what caused the dust, dirt, and hardness. Yet, instead of walking on by, He bends down, picks us up, and holds us in the palm of His hand. God's grace gently uncovers the hurt.

GOD'S GRACE GENTLY UNCOVERS THE HURT. HIS LOVE SMOOTHS OUT THE BROKEN PLACES.

His love smooths out the broken places. And because He never lets us go, we eventually become tumbled right-side up—all brilliant, colorful, and spectacular. Our unique variations uncovered. What was hidden is now gloriously revealed because of Him.

To receive this tumbled, new heart, we must surrender to the process and stay to the end. We can't jump off because the tossing about is too much. Hurt hides. Hurt retreats. It lashes out to be heard and understood. And it self-protects to keep others out.

Love pursues. Love listens and invites us in.

My prayer is that you and I will become transformed to reflect His love to this fallen world. May we persevere with the goal of love in mind, so our edges will be polished and our inner colors will sparkle. This is how our lives become invitations to and testimonies of God's transforming touch.

May the greatest gift of this inside-out transformation be that we're able to see people like Jesus does. Not from a place of pain, but of redemption. I am filled with hope that God will open our hearts for the lost . . . the ones laying by the path unnoticed. Jesus saw them—the multitudes ignored by the religious leaders, the broken woman at the well, the thief on the cross, the despised tax collector in the tree straining for a glimpse of the Messiah. Jesus not only saw them, He reached for them. He loved the unlovable and touched the untouchable.

There are so many people in our lives who long to be seen and known and ultimately touched by the Creator's hand. They want to believe they are worthy of such love. Maybe this is the message your heart needs to hear again too.

When you feel thrown aside or certain that nobody understands you, give your pain to the Lord. He knew the ultimate hurt of betrayal and yet laid down His life for all. There are no rough edges on Him. Just mercy. Just grace. And the beautiful promise to turn tumbled hearts into shining treasures.

You Are So Loved

I will give you a new heart and put a new spirit in you; I will remove from you your heart of stone and give you a heart of flesh.

EZEKIEL 36:26

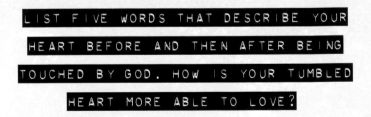

LIST FIVE WORDS THAT DESCRIBE YOUR HEART BEFORE AND THEN AFTER BEING TOUCHED BY GOD. HOW IS YOUR TUMBLED HEART MORE ABLE TO LOVE?

Lord, I've been tossed about by this
upside-down world. Seeing the good
has been hard. Layers of hurt cover
me. But then You pick me up and Your
loving hand smooths away the ugliness
and the rough places that had started
to keep me from joy. Your same hand
also guides and protects me. You
deliver me to safety when I stumble.
On the other side of difficulties
that topple my plans and upend my
life, You dust me off.

I will trust the process of being
tumbled for Your namesake. Have Your
way Lord, so my true colors shine
through for You. Let me see others
as You see them. Help me to love like
You love. In Jesus's name, amen.

Tending to Our Garden

Let my teaching fall like rain
and my words descend like dew,
like showers on new grass,
like abundant rain on
tender plants.

DEUTERONOMY 32:2

I tend a garden, but I don't consider myself a true gardener. I plant in the spring, water when necessary, pull weeds occasionally, cut flowers, and harvest veggies. But I get buried in the specific needs of each plant and get lazy with correct care. There are lots of guidelines and details—where to plant, how to nourish, when to harvest, and so on. I get lost in the weeds, so to speak. The to-do list is long, so I just do what's in front of me. Trying to keep up.

One thing I do know about garden care is that weeds are sneaky and relentless. They disguise themselves. They cozy up next to a plant and make it almost impossible to tell which is the plant and which is the weed. As a result, I'll resist pulling, because I'm unsure, and before you know it, the weed has grown taller than the plant. They completely take over, threatening to snuff out the primary plant's life. The only way to get rid of them is to yank them out by the roots. If you don't, they just grow back stronger than ever.

I've been entangled with weeds of my own over the years. You know the kind. Negative thoughts and emotions that bury a

THE BEAUTIFUL FRUIT OF YOUR LIFE IS WORTH PROTECTING AND SAVING.

little seed in your mind, and before you know it you have an imposter (weed) that looks deceptively like the real thing. Its presence threatens to stifle out the real you. And by "real you," I mean the beautiful plant God intended you to be and grow into—strong, secure, confident, kind, loving, and patient.

My invasive weeds appear often in the form of loneliness. Your invader may be rejection, discontent, fear, anger, depression, or comparison. Maybe it's a toxic relationship or unhealthy habit. Regardless, the undesired seeds that blow in the wind land not only on you but others around you.

So . . . what do you and I do to deal with those weeds?

Identify that it's a weed. It may seem legit, but if it's threatening to choke out the good things in your life, it's a weed! Things that numb, distract, or temporarily lessen pain are substitutes for God's goodness. Still unsure if it's a weed? Identify what you use to numb yourself: food, shopping, show binging, drugs, sex, alcohol, social media, etc. Those things can temporarily satisfy, but they don't get to the root of the problem. In fact, they're a catalyst to the problem!

Take action. Don't wait! Put on your work gloves and start digging. When you reach the roots, don't just snip at the base, because inevitably it will grow back. Dig it all out. It's hard work. You'll get dirty and sweaty, and it will feel futile at times because sure enough, when one gets plucked, another will sprout. But the beautiful fruit of your life is worth protecting and saving.

Prevent its return. In my backyard garden, I prepare the ground by placing black cloth down first and then adding mulch or pine needles over it. In the spiritual realm, you'll need to cover the garden with His Word. Then plant God's seeds of truth to replace the seeds of lies.

Be diligent. Return to the steps each season. You may recognize some weeds that started sprouting in your life when you were young. Many come back as stronger versions of what you first experienced, so strong in fact, that they can no longer be gently pushed aside or ignored. The actions you take now will prevent them from snatching your joy, health, perspective, and hope in the Lord.

With God's help, we can become faithful gardeners who nurture and preserve what is intended to blossom. When we protect our minds and hearts with a thick barrier of His truth, we insulate ourselves with His spoken promises over us. When His lessons become the water and sunlight we crave, we no longer are lost in the weeds, my friend. We are found, saved, and tended to by the Master Gardener.

You Are So Loved

The fruit of the Spirit is love, joy, peace, forbearance, kindness, goodness, faithfulness, gentleness and self-control.

GALATIANS 5:22-23

NOTICE HOW THE FRUIT OF THE SPIRIT IS BLOOMING IN YOU. WHICH ASPECT IS MOST FRAGRANT IN YOUR LIFE'S GARDEN?

Lord, You are the Master Gardener.
You plant beauty in and around me
every day. When I look at nature,
I can't help but feel a bond with
You. You draw us to You through
every living thing. Help me identify
the weeds in my life. Anything that
threatens to choke out the good needs
to go. I am grateful that in and
through You I can do hard things.
I can yank out the roots of things
that don't belong. Show me how to
protect what You are blooming and
growing in my life.

May my garden be a beautiful
reflection of Your grace. Your
goodness. I can do all things
through Christ who strengthens me.
In Jesus's name, amen.

The Beauty of Change

Therefore, if anyone is in Christ, he is a
new creation; old things have passed away;
behold, all things have become new.

2 CORINTHIANS 5:17 NKJV

Have you had one of those "feeling like a failure" days? Your daily challenges present new circumstances, and the new circumstances just feel like too much. Maybe you didn't feel productive enough. Not on top of it enough. Just plain not enough. When do those thoughts and fears grow strong for you? I have journeyed through many times when I didn't feel like I was enough.

As I think about this, the Lord places on my heart the word "change." Am I supposed to share about how hard change is? How we need to change? How the world is changing and we need to be ready? I've been in a constant state of change over the last several years, and it's anything but comfortable. So, I can't tell you it is easy. I continue to feel nervous and on the cusp of something new. I never quite feel up to the task I'm being led toward, and yet here I am facing it again. You are too, whether you realize it or not.

Our lives are full of change. Becoming a wife was a *huge* adjustment for me. I remember waking up to my husband and thinking, *This is it! I have a new title. I'm somebody's wife! His forever partner. That's crazy!*

When our first daughter, Maggie, was born, I was in complete awe that I was a mom. But I also felt overwhelmed . . . this precious life depended on me for everything. I'll never forget coming home from the hospital, looking at my husband, and saying, "I feel like my life is over." Cue the panic attack and a feeling of fear that doubles you over. I know that might sound horrible, but we had waited a very long time to start a family. We had found a comfort zone, a rhythm that worked. Our lives as we knew them *were* over. Things were forever different. Good different, blessed different, but still, entirely different.

Fast-forward to the week we brought home a new puppy we named Favor. On the morning after the first night of cleaning up messes and soothing the little guy, I sat bleary-eyed and barely functioning. That familiar panic of not having what it takes was as strong as the coffee in my cup. He was crawling all over me, whining for attention. I stroked his dependent little head and knew our lives were going to be forever changed. I wondered, *Lord, am I up for this challenge?* Have you ever wondered this too?

We're set in our ways. So even when change is good, it's hard, and even when it's hard, it's good. It stretches us. It's worth the work. The despair that often accompanies transition is temporary. Experiencing change is letting go of old ways and embracing new habits.

We can't do it on our own. Like a pup, we can whine and whimper because it's hard and we are needy, but if we trust the process and let the Lord have His way, a transformation happens.

Visualize a butterfly. Who hasn't paused to watch with awe as one of these amazing creatures gracefully dance in the sky? Yet as we know, they aren't colorful and magnificent and made to flit and float in the beginning. A butterfly starts off as a quirky, unattractive caterpillar. It is so unassuming. Once in the cocoon, a caterpillar is magically transformed into something new.

The same thing happens to us spiritually when we accept Jesus into our lives. The Bible says we are a new creature. Through the renewing of our minds, we can continue on this path of transformation and change without our fear and failings derailing us. Even our thoughts can be transformed. When we worry that we're not enough, we need 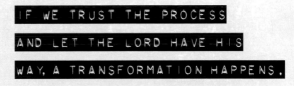 to turn our thoughts back to Jesus and His promises. Surrendering to the cocooning process when we struggle with feeling less than is imperative, so God can transform us into His image. It may be scary, and you may feel ill-equipped to handle the process of learning and letting go, but friend, God will give you everything you need to change.

It's time to burst forth and let the world see His beauty and light in you. It's so worth it.

You Are So Loved

We are God's handiwork, created in Christ
Jesus to do good works, which God
prepared in advance for us to do.

EPHESIANS 2:10

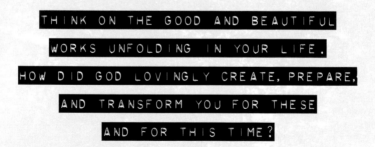

THINK ON THE GOOD AND BEAUTIFUL
WORKS UNFOLDING IN YOUR LIFE.
HOW DID GOD LOVINGLY CREATE, PREPARE,
AND TRANSFORM YOU FOR THESE
AND FOR THIS TIME?

Lord, Your sacrifice and grace allow me to be a new creation. Even when I face spiritual struggles, I know the battle is already won. The work is done. I've been changed!

Grant me the strength to do whatever You call me to do. When I start a new endeavor, I will press through the overwhelm so the pursuit produces fruit that pleases You. Thank You for the worthy challenges ahead that renew me again and again.

When I'm tempted to cocoon in doubt rather than in Your love and power, remind me that it's not time to hide but to break forth and be changed into Your image. May I become a beautiful butterfly, drawing others to You.
In Jesus's name I pray. Amen.

Rest Easy

Come to me, all you who are weary and burdened, and I will give you rest. Take my yoke upon you and learn from me, for I am gentle and humble in heart, and you will find rest for your souls. For my yoke is easy and my burden is light.

MATTHEW 11:28-30

When you think of your lists of things to do and your responsibilities, do you feel the pressure? The weight of such burdens?

I love the imagery used in the Bible of Jesus asking us to share His yoke. A yoke is something that is put on work animals, like oxen, to pull a load. So, Jesus was referring to a heavy piece of wood that would lay across an animal's shoulders to pull a load. In our humanity we load up with the worries and cares of the day, and our figurative yokes become too heavy and difficult to carry. When we take our heaviness to Him, His gentleness lessens our burden. It takes the pressure off our shoulders and places it on His. His yoke is easy, and His burden is light. Hallelujah! That imagery of this transfer is beautiful and comforting. Take a second and envision lifting a heavy weight off your own shoulders and placing it on His. Maybe it's a painful past, a health trial, a heartache you just can't seem to let go of. Give it to Him.

The Bible talks a lot about rest. The Sabbath, the day of rest, is referred to many times as a command. God rested. We must rest. It not only restores our physical bodies, it realigns our minds. But I'm not great at following this guideline. I'm a striver. I hate to admit it, but I have to-do lists a mile long. I'm sure you do too! I go from one big project to another without so much as a sigh or an appreciative high-five to myself for the accomplishment. I push myself to the point of burnout, and it's only then that I take a rest. It's a forced rest. A means to an end.

The Bible's message protects us from burnout by showing us how to step back. Jesus craved solitude and sought out places of quiet to regroup and gain strength. He'd set out by boat, head to the desert, or walk in the gardens to take time away. Once He was distanced from the crowds, He found peace in praying to His Father, gaining insight and direction.

God, in His beautiful role as Creator, took six days to create all the things, and then as another act of creation—one that was included in the number of days to create—He rested. I think it's fascinating the Bible mentions that day of rest. It didn't have to be recorded. It could have been just another day in the multitude of days, but it was mentioned as an example for how we are to live. Even God carved out time to rest. In Genesis 2, God blessed that seventh day and called it holy. Taking time to rest is holy! It's a sacred act and pleases the Lord.

On the trip to France with my daughter, we drove back roads through lush fields of poppies. Orange happy faces swayed in the breeze and beckoned me to stop and pay attention. Have you noticed that even the beauty of His creation invites us to rest? Are there things in your everyday surroundings that might be inviting you to lean in and look more closely?

At home we have bird feeders and a fountain on our back patio. The sound of bubbling

HAVE YOU NOTICED THAT EVEN THE BEAUTY OF HIS CREATION INVITES US TO REST?

water transports me to my happy place. It helps me to stop spinning, and it quiets my tumbling thoughts. The birdsong brings me joy. When the two are blended, I'm completely transported to a place of peace and calm. Even though it's not an entire day of Sabbath, it's a Sabbath moment, and we need those too. We have to actively search them out and fold them into the fabric of our every day. Rest is vital. It's an act of surrender. It's a laying down and a conscious decision to be like Him, not only in our busy full lives devoted to His glory, but in those places of quiet and reflection, seeking His face. I'm ready to enter that place of rest. Are you?

You Are So Loved

Because so many people were coming and going that they did not even have a chance to eat, he said to them, "Come with me by yourselves to a quiet place and get some rest."

MARK 6:31

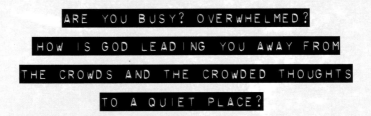

ARE YOU BUSY? OVERWHELMED? HOW IS GOD LEADING YOU AWAY FROM THE CROWDS AND THE CROWDED THOUGHTS TO A QUIET PLACE?

Thank You, Lord, for Your promise to give me rest. You see me in all my human weakness and striving, and You offer to take my burdens and make them lighter for me. Help me notice the fields of the flowers, the birds, and the wind in the trees. Give me patience to pause and see Your hand in everything.

Lord, in the quiet places, You speak to my heart and align it with Yours once again. Forgive me for trying to move ahead of what You have called me to. I give over all my striving, goals, and to-do lists and lay them at Your feet. As I take on Your easy and light yoke, I feel the renewal You offer. In Jesus's name, amen.

Joy Comes

**Weeping may stay for the night,
but rejoicing comes in the morning.**

PSALM 30:5

My deep feelings began as a child. I spent a lot of time in the nurse's room at school. Stress would manifest as an upset stomach. In grade school I even spent a night in the hospital to have tests run. The results were inconclusive, but the truth was clear—anxiety from underlying family tensions were entangled in my mind, body, and spirit.

Years later, depression came to me as a young mama. My three-and-a-half-year-old, Maggie, was right in the middle of toddlerhood. I was pregnant with my second daughter. The bedtime routine with Maggie had turned into kicking and screaming sessions. This wasn't ideal for a tired, hormonal mama. Those months were hard. I struggled with rage and knew I was disciplining out of anger and frustration more than not. I felt hopeless and ended up taking antidepressants for a season. The side effects kept me praying for another way. I had times where it lifted. But it made its presence known again when winter hit.

We had just moved to Minnesota. The winters were brutally

cold, dark, and long. Going out to run errands with the kids was overwhelming. While standing in line at the grocery store, weariness nearly consumed me as I thought through all the steps ahead: bag the groceries, get them to the car, load them, unload them and the girls, and once home, put the groceries away. I stood in the parking lot trying to catch my breath. I'd never worried about freezing to death trying to load groceries before. But on that day, with tears streaming down my face, I knew that exposure could kill.

Have you endured times when simple errands seemed insurmountable?

The only place I wanted to be was the only place I felt warm—under my electric blanket in bed, sleeping. Many days I would feed the girls breakfast, set them in front of the TV, and go back to bed. It's painful to confess, but this is what my season of weeping and weariness looked like. Then when a family member became ill and road trips to and from Illinois were added to 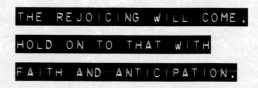 the mix, I ended up in the ER with chest pains. It was an anxiety attack. From then on panic came when life felt out of control.

To ease the ache, I started connecting with others through blogging. Reading stories and blog posts that resonated with me encouraged me to start my own blog and it became my lifeline. I'd take pictures, talk about my life, and in doing so, I found and shared beauty and purpose. The feelings of isolation left. Writing down my thoughts trained me to look for the good. The Lord started revealing Himself to me through the ordinary. I couldn't write without declaring and celebrating what life meant in and through Him.

My depression eventually lifted, and He opened the door for me to create professionally.

Have you been walking in a season of weeping too? The rejoicing will come. Hold onto that with faith and anticipation. Here are actions that help me.

move and sweat	practice self-care
learn	journal
write a letter	create
pray	notice nature
praise God	plan a coffee date
unplug	schedule a spa visit

In those dark moments, you are never alone. Even the Bible greats struggled at times with a season of weeping. David did when he was on the run from Saul. (Psalm 42 captures David pouring out his aching soul before the Lord.) Job did when there wasn't a corner of his world that hadn't been devastated. (His shattered heart is laid bare in Job 3.) Moses did when he struggled with managing the Israelites. (Numbers 11 shares his overwhelmed plea.)

Morning *will* come. Opportunities to rejoice *will* arise. The joy of the Lord *will* fall on you and He *will* give you strength. I know because we're never left alone in the dark. The Lord is always with us and for us.

You Are So Loved

There is a time for everything, and a season
for every activity under the heavens . . .
a time to weep and a time to laugh, a time
to mourn and a time to dance.

ECCLESIASTES 3:1,4

IF YOU ARE HEAVY-HEARTED, DESCRIBE
HOW IT FEELS TO KNOW THAT THERE
WILL, ONCE AGAIN, BE A TIME FOR
LAUGHTER, JOY, AND DANCING.

Lord, You have been with me through emotionally, physically, and spiritually dark times. Thank You for never leaving me alone in the hard places. When it is difficult to see the good or notice beauty, You refresh my spirit enough for me to truly grasp the ordinary blessings so I can join in the rejoicing of a new morning. You give me strength for today's needs. You turn my eye to the little things that refocus my heart toward joy.

I will rejoice even when I can't see the whole picture and the changes ahead. I will rejoice because I know I'm not alone. Thank You for hearing my prayers whether they are through tears or smiles.
In Jesus's name, amen.

The Great Gathering

Concerning the coming of our Lord Jesus
Christ and our being gathered to him . . .

THESSALONIANS 2:1

I was driving home the other night and witnessed a starling murmuration. Have you ever seen one? You would definitely remember it. Thousands of black birds moving in unison, changing direction quickly, forming shapes in the sky. It's like seeing a miracle with your own eyes. It doesn't seem possible. As you watch in awe, you can't help but wonder: *Who's in charge? Who's directing the surges and swells?*

The same hand that guides these breathtaking flocks in their mesmerizing formations is the hand that gathers and guides us. Let that sink in for a minute.

That beautiful display reminded me of the great gathering that will be in Jesus's presence. I don't know if you can relate, but sometimes the stressors of this temporal world bring an indescribable heaviness to my spirit. How do we live knowing that our time here is uncertain? How do we exist when a change of season is nipping at our heels and a big move is imminent?

The assurance of heaven restores my hope and fills me with expectancy for being a part of this future gathering. During times of uncertainty or waiting, we must be faithful in our pursuit of what matters. Our time on this earth is not given to us to be wasted or wished away.

Set your mind on hope. One of my favorite hymns is "Turn Your Eyes upon Jesus." My heart resonates with its lyrics of how things of the earth and the material world will grow dim when held up to the light of God's glory. Yes! That is how I feel. Sometimes I look around at the world and even with its beauty and wonder, I feel less and less like this is where I belong. My heart and soul long for my spiritual home.

Colossians 3:2 (ESV) says, "Set your minds on things that are above, not on things that are on earth." When I get discouraged about temporary matters, deadlines, and the pressure I place on myself to do well, that verse soothes me and I feel the shift. Do you? Does it bring you a sense of balance  as you ponder both heaven and earth? We are here. We're called to stay present on the path God has for us. Sharing the good news is our common direction. Witnessing is the way we increase the gathering and become more than we can be on our own.

Do you feel torn between worlds? Are you on high alert for His glorious return? Allow yourself to rest in the hope of heaven while walking daily in God's presence. Then, when the unnecessary and temporary burdens and frets are fading, you'll have that much more energy and focus to give to what is necessary and eternal. Don't get discouraged.

Unite. I know for a fact that the enemy comes to steal, kill, and destroy (John 10:10). People will become divided and divisive and there is turmoil and ruin left in the wake of such conflict. That is why unity in the body of believers is so important. Let's set our differences aside. Our loud opinions and our need to be right only cause division. Let's not let the spirit of offense take root and rob us of a chance to work together for God's purposes. Now is the time to come together and move as one. One body, moving in love, becoming a miracle that can be seen with the naked eye. Together we are impressive. Together we can make a difference and soar with power! The world will stop and stare because we will move, obey, and transform as one body of believers.

Awe came over me as I watched those birds move in unison. His infinite beauty and creation on display for all to see. I hope that maybe the next time you see a murmuration, you'll pause with the same revelation. We are the body . . . let's unite and flow as one under the One.

You Are So Loved

Therefore encourage one another and build each other up, just as in fact you are doing.

THESSALONIANS 5:11

CHOOSE ONE WAY TO LOOK AT YOUR CIRCUMSTANCES WITH HOPE AND ONE WAY TO BUILD UP A PERSON IN YOUR LIFE.

Lord, prepare me for the greatest
gathering that has ever been.
Direct my flight path and help me
to persevere. May I bring glory and
honor to Your name and have the
strength to finish strong. I'm so
excited for Your return. Use me to
gather others so they too can marvel
at Your goodness and grace and be
in Your presence.

Give all Your children increased
boldness. Keep us from distraction.
Lord, when Your trumpet sounds may
our eyes be fixed on You. I cannot
wait for that day when I will see You
face to face. And until then, I will
gladly pay attention, be present,
and seek unity. I love You, Lord.
In Jesus's name I pray, amen.

The Thorn

Cast your cares on the Lord and he will
sustain you; he will never let the
righteous be shaken.

PSALM 55:22

Do you have a thorn? A consistent source of pain that you've learned to live with or ignore? Would you be surprised to know it can become a source of faith? Of deeper belief?

The morning after we signed contracts for our fixer-upper— remember the one we bought online?—I awakened with a loud ringing in my ears. A never-ending roar that increased in quiet times. I thought it would go away. Maybe I had come down with something? Maybe it was a virus or head cold? I quickly fell down the rabbit hole of researching it. I went to a doctor, who suggested hearing aids! I prayed (a lot). I fought hopelessness. Panic would come at me—especially at night, when the sound would be almost deafening. I pleaded with God to make it stop. That was more than five years ago. It never left.

Instead of an instant healing, there has been a progression of learning to tune it out. I've become so used to the noise in my head that it's a normal part of my life now. I get busy during the day and forget about it. While it remains, the panic I felt thinking it would never leave is gone.

When I can no longer ignore the noise, the Holy Spirit reminds me to ask for healing. I have anointing oil on my bathroom vanity, and I anoint my head and pray for healing often. I'm a firm believer that God heals, because Jesus healed all the wounded and broken people He encountered. But the truth is that healing doesn't always come when or how we want it.

Sometimes we walk with a "thorn," such as the one the apostle Paul described:

> *So if I want to boast, I won't do so as a fool because I will be speaking the truth. But I will stop there, since I don't want to be credited with anything except exactly what people see and hear from me. To keep me grounded and stop me from becoming too high and mighty due to the extraordinary character of these revelations, I was given a thorn in the flesh—a nagging nuisance of Satan, a messenger to plague me!*
>
> 2 CORINTHIANS 12:6-7, VOICE

The Bible doesn't say what Paul's thorn was, but apparently it was a clear source of pain and frustration. A physical thorn in nature is a sharp extension of a plant that serves to defend the creation. I don't believe God gives us suffering. I believe we live in a fallen world and sickness comes. But He can use those "thorns," and in turn, a deeper dependency on Him can grow. Each point of anguish causes us to lean in closer to the Lord's presence. In my case, I am led to pray more often and with a greater sense of dependence on God.

Your ongoing source of grief could be shaping your life to become a needed example of walking through hard things with faith.

I'm always looking for the lesson. I'm always asking the Lord what I should be learning from any given circumstance.

Here's what I do know. I haven't given up praying for a miracle regarding my personal healing, because the Bible says, "You do not have because you do not ask God" (James 4:2), and we are supposed to petition for things. He hears us, and if it lines up with His will, 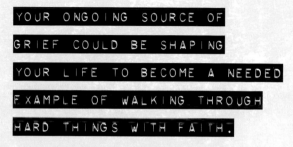 it will happen. I know He can take the ringing from me instantly, so I keep asking. I keep believing in faith, and when my healing happens, I'll be shouting it from the mountain tops.

YOUR ONGOING SOURCE OF GRIEF COULD BE SHAPING YOUR LIFE TO BECOME A NEEDED EXAMPLE OF WALKING THROUGH HARD THINGS WITH FAITH.

I'm thankful that despite the thorn, God is clearly with me in my need and daily life. My gratitude has grown rather than diminished. He's taken the sting out of the pain and given me the grace to live with it.

So what is your thorn? Is it something physical or environmental that causes you pain daily? I don't presume to fully understand God and His ways, but I do know that in His wisdom He sorts out what is best for our lives, because He loves us and is for us. In the midst of the hurt, we are called to bold, fervent prayer, making our requests known. He calls us to trust and believe that He sees the things that hurt us, and to know if they don't go away, there's a plan in place.

You Are So Loved

Let us then approach God's throne of grace with confidence, so that we may receive mercy and find grace to help us in our time of need.

HEBREWS 4:16

PRAY TO BRING YOUR WOUNDS, YOUR THORNS, TO GOD. WHAT DOES IT FEEL LIKE TO EXCHANGE THEM FOR GOD'S MERCY AND JOY?

Lord, thank You that I can come to You and lay my burdens at Your feet. I'm grateful that I can ask and petition for my desires. I trust that You hear me! I boldly pray Your perfect will and believe that You know exactly what I need. Give me strength, wisdom, and endurance when I am tempted to turn to anger or sink into sorrow because of my personal thorn. Help me to see the good, because every good gift comes from You.

Help me to see the plan You have. And for the parts I cannot see, give me the faith to trust all that You are and all that You are doing in me. I love You, Lord.
In Jesus's name, amen.

Salt + Light

Let your light shine before others,
that they may see your good deeds and
glorify your Father in heaven.

MATTHEW 5:16

Have you ever said something, created something, or planned something and then later, in hindsight, the deeper reason for it became clear? And the purpose was so much richer and more beautiful than you could ever have guessed?

I painted this accompanying image with my sole focus on the swans. The lily pads were just filler. But when I looked back on the image much later, the Lord surprisingly redirected my full attention to the lily pads. Did you know that water lilies' roots lie in the deep places? The tuber is buried in the dark, and it has to send shoots up as lily pad leaves to act as solar panels to collect light and oxygen to survive. The tuber would never grow if it didn't push through the darkness and rise to the surface to gather strength from the sun.

This past year has beaten my spirits down. My heart has grown a bit cold, and I feel like hiding and staying to myself. My previous eagerness to reach out and share about life now just felt like adding to the world's noise. Then the Lord directed me to this.

> *You are the salt of the earth. But if the salt loses its saltiness, how can it be made salty again? It is no longer good for anything, except to be thrown out and trampled underfoot. You are the light of the world. A town built on a hill cannot be hidden. Neither do people light a lamp and put it under a bowl. Instead they put it on its stand, and it gives light to everyone in the house.*

MATTHEW 5:13–15

As the words of that Scripture spoke to my heart, I was reminded that this dark world needs us. If we stay buried and hidden, nobody will see the beauty and abundance that a life with Christ provides.

We are set apart and beloved. We can keep that to ourselves . . . or we can allow the Holy Spirit to use us in our vulnerability with discernment and wisdom, guiding our footsteps in a purposeful way. When we push down fear, doubt, pride, and selfishness, and take brave steps into the uncomfortable place of obedience, the reward will be great. It's a life of living beyond self. Friend, we're so lucky to have this opportunity to love others and speak forth things that encourage, set people free, and bring them to Christ. Walking in influence and "setting up our lamps" to be seen is our calling.

As I gazed into the lily pad's background, I realized its purpose reaches beyond its capacity to care for itself. It also provides helpful bacteria, keeps the water's temperature cool, gives shelter to fish, and provides protection from predators for the frog. The light and oxygen it gathers not only make the water lily bloom with beauty but also benefit everything in the pond.

Jesus's words for His disciples at the Sermon on the Mount were meant for us too. We are to be salt and light. What is even more remarkable is that we don't have to strive to be salt and light. Jesus declared that we *are* salt and light.

Salt is a preservative. It makes food taste better. It increases thirst. It's imperative in living as a disciple. We make people thirsty for Him.

Light is easily seen in the darkness. When we are the light of Christ to the world, it requires us to be visible. Influential. I  don't like that trendy word, but it's true. He places us in a position of influence, and that means even when we don't feel like it, we are able to push through our darkness or the comfort of our hiding place and surface with beauty. With hope. With light.

Are you ready to push through the murk and rise to the top? To "solar panel" up and gather and reflect the light of the Son into this dark world? You are! I know you are.

You Are So Loved

You were once darkness, but now you are light
in the Lord. Live as children of light.

EPHESIANS 5:8

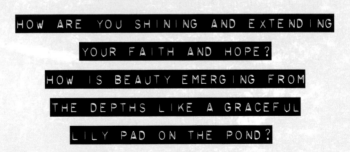

HOW ARE YOU SHINING AND EXTENDING
YOUR FAITH AND HOPE?
HOW IS BEAUTY EMERGING FROM
THE DEPTHS LIKE A GRACEFUL
LILY PAD ON THE POND?

Thank You, Lord, for shedding Your
light on me so I can reflect it and
Your love to those around me. Help me
make good decisions based on wisdom
and discernment from the Holy Spirit.
Guide my thoughts so I can reframe
how I look at and care for this world
when it seems scary. Show me how to
make my way through the dark to
the surface where I can be both
salt and light.

There are so many people who need
love, grace, and Your transforming
touch. I boldly ask for influence and
then the courage and faith to serve
in that area of influence.
Use me. Draw people to me, Lord,
so I can point them to You.
In Jesus's name, amen.

Journey to Restoration

Let my passion for life be restored,
tasting joy in every breakthrough you
bring to me. Hold me close to you
with a willing spirit that obeys
whatever you say.

PSALM 51:12 TPT

We didn't vacation much as a family when I was young, but I fondly remember driving across the country from Illinois to visit my grandparents in Arizona. My parents loaded our old blue Chevy Impala to the brim, and my brothers and I crammed into the backseat. It was a very long, uncomfortable trip. But those endless hours of driving through the desert forged a deep bond with the West and its arid climate, otherworldly cactus, and distant mountains. It seemed magical.

Thoughts of the desert stir my mind to wonder what the wilderness looked like when the Israelites wandered around for 40 years. Even though they were enslaved in Egypt, it was familiar to them. Yet, deliverance from bondage wasn't the easy road they thought it would be. When faced with uncertainty, they quickly replaced faith in God with fear. They constructed idols and worshipped false gods. They became restless and complained nonstop. They tried and failed to hoard God's provision of daily manna. Repeatedly they relied on their own instincts and means of survival instead of trusting in the Lord's care.

We think of restoration as getting back to where we were. But God's restoration is different. He blesses His people for their faith in hard

WE MUST PROTECT OUR PEACE AND GUARD OUR HEARTS AT ALL COSTS.

times by more than making up for what they've lost. There are many powerful stories in the Bible. I think of Job who was tested and lost everything, and Joseph who was horribly mistreated by his family and sold into slavery. (Joseph eventually became second only to the king.) And of course, the Israelites in the desert. The most important story of restoration is that as sinners we are given abundant grace through Christ. We are restored to relationship and communion with God.

In Scripture, often situations are at their most dire when God steps in and turns things right-side up. We discover that for the Israelites and for us, the road to restoration involves a few actions.

Put God in His place. When things are going sideways, my first response is to run to the phone to call my mom or a friend to ease my pain and gain instruction on what to do. For comfort, I might post on social media, indulge in a shopping spree, or watch Netflix. But God is the only source who knows and loves me, and He is longing to be my first choice when I'm hurting and broken. He's a jealous God and when we put people or things in place of Him, it only delays the healing. And let's face it, it's idolatry.

Repent. James 4:17 warns us, "Anyone, then, who knows the right thing to do, yet fails to do it, is guilty of sin" (BSB). Sin has become a dirty word to many because it seems harsh and judgmental, but sin is simply separation. Not on God's part, as nothing can separate us from His love. Yet sin can make *us* feel distant and prevent us from deeper intimacy with the Father. The finished work of the cross is our pass to joy, peace, and love. Humbly asking for forgiveness makes things right and leads us to a place of restoration and strength.

Get quiet and listen. Our modern world is extremely noisy. It screams at us to look every which way. It tells us what to think, feel, say, and do. We must protect our peace and guard our hearts at all costs. This requires discernment. Getting quiet is imperative to hearing from the Lord, and hearing from the Lord is vital for the healing of whatever needs restoring.

Have a thankful heart. Reading about the Israelites stumbling around in the wilderness is the only example I need to see to understand what an ungrateful heart is and does. It hardens. It blinds. It robs us of the miracles around us. When we start counting our joys and being thankful for the multitude of ways the Lord blesses us and cares for us every day, something changes. Doubts dissipate. All of life's inevitable disappointments, hurts, and hardships start to lessen so healing can unfold.

Let your journey to restoration begin!

You Are So Loved

He restores my soul; he leads me in
the paths of righteousness.

PSALM 23:3 NKJV

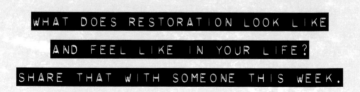

WHAT DOES RESTORATION LOOK LIKE
AND FEEL LIKE IN YOUR LIFE?
SHARE THAT WITH SOMEONE THIS WEEK.

Lord, I know that even as a
believer, there will be times when
circumstances feel like too much.
Times when darkness will threaten my
faith. May I quickly reclaim my trust
that You are always for me. You long
for my restoration and draw me near
when I've strayed from Your path.
You're the one I will run to when
doubts or fears sneak in. I will make
You first in my life as my comforter,
source of peace, and Savior.

God, You call me to trust Your
provision and care. When I do, I
am more dependent on You and Your
grace. I praise You for spiritual
restoration beyond what I could have
imagined on the desert road.
You make life better than before.
In Jesus's name, amen.

Diving into New Territory

God-Enthroned spoke to me and said,
"Consider this! I am making everything
to be new and fresh."

REVELATION 21:5 TPT

Have you ever had a difficult change you initially resisted or grieved that became the exact transition God used to set you on the best path?

Many years ago, I had a breakup with a close friend. Out of nowhere a heated discussion severed a bond I thought could never be broken. It took me a while to realize that God had *allowed* that discussion to happen. Unknowingly, I had put that friendship on a pedestal and He had other plans for me. Ultimately, that friendship was holding me back.

I'm loyal. When you're my person I hold on for dear life. So the hurt from that breakup, and several other friendships that had waned over the years, caused me insecurity with being vulnerable and letting people get close. Not understanding what went wrong kept me stuck in a pattern of feeling rejected until recently when God revealed that He was the Author of those transitions. In that particular instance, if the relationship hadn't changed, I never would have been open to a cross-country move—a move that was necessary for the growth of my future business, ministry, and creative joy.

The truth is we get comfortable. Same routines. Same relationships.

It's easy to fall into a set way of doing things. When God called Moses to lead the Israelites out of Egypt, Moses responded with reluctance. He was content living in the wilderness tending sheep, but God had *new territory* in mind. Moses didn't feel capable or qualified. His excuses of "Who am I? What if they don't believe me? I'm not eloquent enough" didn't deter God. God had a plan, and He gave him the tools to complete the task, but it took a willing heart from Moses to obey the Lord (Exodus 3).

GOD GIVES US A NEW SONG, A NEW JOY WHEN HE HAS US MOVE FORWARD IN HIS PURPOSE AND PLAN FOR US.

What about Esther? Just a normal Jewish girl, she was hand-picked from obscurity to live in the King's harem. A place that must have felt so uncomfortable and unfamiliar. She was taken from the only life she knew and placed in *new territory*. She had to let go of the old life in order for God to use her in the new one. Both Moses and Esther were used to save the Jewish people. If *you* have a willing heart, just think of how God can and will use you!

Maybe you are being ushered into a new territory and that move requires obedience in the form of a loose grip and a willingness to trust. God is shaping our days even when we can't understand where He is leading us. When we submit to His plan, we won't get lost in the emotional confusion that can accompany change. We will be moved to follow the One who knows us intimately and loves us more than we could ever comprehend.

What scares you about the new thing happening? Think about how it has unfolded and how God has impressed on your heart certain truths or given you certain strengths to prepare for this very thing. God doesn't push us toward new territory without a plan. And He certainly doesn't lead us there to be left all alone.

I have a sweet memory of a whale-watching tour our family took in Hawaii. At one point, the captain dropped a microphone into the ocean and within seconds we could hear whale song. I was surprised to see a young man burst into tears at the sound. Hearing God's creation sing from the depths was such a moving spiritual experience. I'll never forget it. I discovered that whales change their song when entering new territory to resemble the other whales. The previous patterns of its song never reoccurred. God gives them a new song for their new territory. And in our lives, I believe God gives us a new song, a new joy when He has us move forward in His purpose and plan for us.

Only the Master Conductor of our lives can create our unique melody. When we listen, praise, pray, and ultimately obey, saying, "Lord, have Your way . . . let my life be a beautiful symphony," the world will be moved. They will hear His song, and it will call them to join you in the deep places. Let's be willing to dive into that new territory. It's time.

You Are So Loved

He put a new song in my mouth, a hymn of praise to our God. Many will see and fear the LORD and put their trust in him.

PSALM 40:3

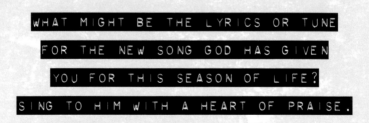

WHAT MIGHT BE THE LYRICS OR TUNE FOR THE NEW SONG GOD HAS GIVEN YOU FOR THIS SEASON OF LIFE? SING TO HIM WITH A HEART OF PRAISE.

Thank You, Lord, for reminding me
in Your Word that You direct my path
every single day. Even when I don't
understand why things happen, You do,
and You're directing me. Continue
to give me wisdom and discernment
going forward. Help me hold tightly
to Your ways as I hold loosely to the
circumstances of this world.

Release me from the hurt from
previous relationships or things I
can't comprehend. Reveal Your plan,
so I have closure toward the past
and am open to the new territory You
bring me into. Because of You, I have
a song to sing. I promise to open my
mouth, mind, and heart to be a vessel
of glory and honor for Your name
forever. In Jesus's name, amen.

Sweet Surrender

The LORD will guide you always; he will
satisfy your needs in a sun-scorched land
and will strengthen your frame. You will
be like a well-watered garden, like a
spring whose waters never fail.

ISAIAH 58:11

Gazing out the back patio doors of the house we were touring, I knew instantly that I was standing in our new home. Even though the house was in a subdivision, it overlooked the most beautiful farm with rolling hills, a giant red barn, and cows! Every night, I'd sit in suburbia and wistfully gaze out at the farm life I'd always wanted. From my deck I could hear the cow calls, smell the manure, tune into the clang of the distant dinner bell. With eager anticipation, I awaited dinnertime—my favorite part of the day—to soak in that view and relax. Is there anything better than watching cows run for their evening meal?

The only thing that tainted those moments was the flood of worries about the future.

From the minute we moved in until the moment we moved out seven years later, I worried that our road would get too busy, that the farm would be sold, and that a developer would take away our beloved view. Please tell me I'm not the only one who worries about things out of my control? I have a tendency to do that. All it takes is a rumor, a headline, or a gossip to get my wheels turning and I focus on the worse-case scenario. My peace goes right out the window . . . or sometimes, a patio door!

I'm years away from that memory. I'm sitting on my own hill, with my own farm now. A life I've always dreamed of. I even have a big, red barn that houses my art studio. It's dreamy, and yet worry still weaves its way into the crevices of my mind. We live next to 100 acres of prime real estate, and "for sale" signs are at every turn in my picturesque small town. Everything seems to be changing rapidly; therefore, I plot and plan about planting trees and building fences and trying to preserve what I hold dear. But the truth is, none of it is mine and none of it is in my control. Gracious! That's a hard pill to swallow.

Isn't it amazing that the things we hold close are the things that constantly evolve  and change? Our parents get older. Our kids grow up and move out. Our bodies age and become something unfamiliar. It all requires a loose hold and an open heart.

Despite my struggle with a tight grip, I can honestly say the second I decide to surrender, an unraveling occurs. Because I've often wrestled with worrying over circumstances that I can't control, I've had to practice the act of surrender often. Try it with me. Imagine your hand opening up and say these words, "Lord, I give it all back to You. I trust You. Your will be done." Those last words, "Your will be done," create the ultimate prayer. I want nothing more than His will, not mine. So, if the worst things I can imagine actually happen, my heart will be softened because I prayed His perfect will. I have peace because I trust that He knows what is best for my life.

The antidote for worry is always prayer. I've felt this time and again in my own life. I can be all tied up in my bubble of anxiety and I'll call my mama, and she'll immediately start to pray. Or something will be going sideways with work and my helper Meg, who is an instantaneous prayer warrior, will grab my hands and we'll take it to the Lord. The act of acknowledging Him and asking for His help and guidance creates a place and mindset of trust. This action initiates a great big sigh of surrender as it positions Him in charge of all the things that take up room in my mind. Prayer is like a sweet aroma drifting to heaven. It aligns everything and it's something I need to do more often.

Our God is the God of angel armies. He knows our needs. He is the supplier of our everything. His Word is the well that will never dry out. He's the quencher of our thirsty souls. Those cows that I watched go to dinner nightly? They reminded me of Psalm 50:10-11, "Every animal of the forest is mine, and the cattle on a thousand hills. I know every bird in the mountains, and the insects in the fields are mine." He owns everything, including my heart, so why would I waste a second worrying about a thing?

You Are So Loved

Peace I leave with you; my peace I give you.
I do not give to you as the world gives.
Do not let your hearts be troubled
and do not be afraid.

JOHN 14:27

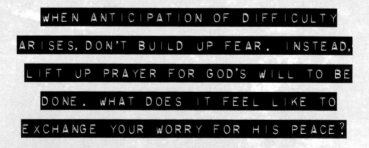

WHEN ANTICIPATION OF DIFFICULTY
ARISES, DON'T BUILD UP FEAR. INSTEAD,
LIFT UP PRAYER FOR GOD'S WILL TO BE
DONE. WHAT DOES IT FEEL LIKE TO
EXCHANGE YOUR WORRY FOR HIS PEACE?

Thank You, Lord, for giving me access to Your throne room. Forgive me for trying to be my own God at times by picking up worry and trying to control things. That's not my job. I love that You are the God of abundance . . . there is no lack in You. When I worry about my daily needs, I am reminded that You are my provider. My heart turns to You with faith and gratitude.

Fill my thirsty soul from the well that will never go dry. I want Your will above my own in every area. When signs and happenings indicate change is coming, may my first response be to pray. And may my whole self say, "Have Your way, Lord!" In Jesus's name I pray, amen.

High Hopes

Why, my soul, are you downcast?
Why so disturbed within me? Put your
hope in God, for I will yet praise him,
my Savior and my God.

PSALM 42:5

Is your hope tank running low these days?

Recently I saw the phrase "high hopes" and it made me think of a show I loved when I was a little girl, *Laverne & Shirley*. If the characters were ever discouraged, Shirley would sing the song "High Hopes" about a little ant carrying a rubber tree plant. In no time, Laverne's attitude and outlook would be on the upswing.

Did you know that the expression "high hopes" means having an expectation that something very good or successful will happen?

When life comes at us hard—and let's face it, it seems hard a lot of the time—we can easily forget to be filled with hope. When we are in the weeds of heaviness, our hope and expectation for good gets blurry. When fear sneaks in, when tragedy strikes, when bad news burdens us, our focus often shifts to the circumstances.

Have you lost focus on where your hope is? When you place  your hope in the Lord, you will know where to look, where to turn, and where to find your peace during difficult times. Nobody can take that away from you. These perspective shifts will keep your hopes high when you encounter the lows.

Remember that this world is not our home. When pressures rise, hold onto the promises and truth of God's Word, "This world is not our permanent home; we are looking forward to a home yet to come" (Hebrews 13:14 NLT). Your crisis or heartache is not the end of the story. We will have trials and tribulations, but God has already overcome them. Take comfort knowing that the thing that feels insurmountable now is temporary, because this life is a blink in the big picture. Remind yourself of forever, and it will make the everything that is temporal shift in priority.

Know that everything we see is not all there is. There is a natural world that looks a certain way. Circumstances seem like concrete reality, but there is a spiritual realm that we cannot see. The Bible says we wrestle not against flesh and blood, but against principalities and darkness (Ephesians 6:12). It also says that "greater is He who is in you than he who is in the world" (1 John 4:4 NASB). Even though we cannot see it, there is a plan in place that is for our good.

When we are obedient and faithful, God works through us to give us hope and to give Him glory. "The LORD will again delight in you and make you prosperous . . . if you obey the LORD your God and keep his commands and decrees that are written in this Book of the Law and turn to the LORD your God with all your heart and with all your soul" (Deuteronomy 30:9-10). If progress feels elusive, know that your efforts won't go unseen. His unseen work will be known one day. Trust that God is for you and claim His promises.

Turn your eyes upon Jesus. This is a literal perspective shift. It is so easy to only look at our troubles, our inabilities, or our past mistakes. When our eyes are on Jesus, we see His reflection, and our doubts about our own identity and value will dissolve. We won't dwell on the hard times when our gaze is set upward on Him.

> *We wait in hope for the LORD; he is our help and our shield. In him our hearts rejoice, for we trust in his holy name. May your unfailing love be with us, LORD, even as we put our hope in you.*
>
> PSALM 33:20-22

With confidence, we can look to Jesus and wait in hope for Him, for He is our help and protection. He is the source of our blessings, strength, and contentment. His Word flows with these promises, my friend, and reminds us that when things are falling apart, "God is our refuge and strength, an ever-present help in trouble" (Psalm 46:1). Our safe place is in His presence, always and forever.

You may be reading this and thinking, *But you don't know my life. You don't know what I'm walking through.* I don't, but He does! And your every hope is in Him.

You Are So Loved

May the God of hope fill you with all joy
and peace as you trust in him, so that
you may overflow with hope by the
power of the Holy Spirit.

ROMANS 15:13

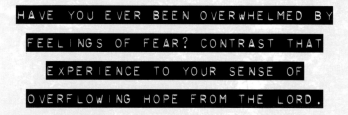

HAVE YOU EVER BEEN OVERWHELMED BY
FEELINGS OF FEAR? CONTRAST THAT
EXPERIENCE TO YOUR SENSE OF
OVERFLOWING HOPE FROM THE LORD.

Heavenly Daddy, thank You for the high hopes I have in You. I will not trade my great expectations of good things to come for a human fear of the future. Despite what the world says or what my circumstances look like, I'll turn my eyes to You, Lord, with hope. Why waste time fretting about my situation or those who might be against me? Nothing and no one can separate me from Your love.
You're in my corner.

Thank You for prospering me, protecting me, guiding me. You take care of my every need as I face what's yet to come. I'm excited to see what's in store! I trust You with my today and all my tomorrows.
In Jesus's name, amen.

The Scent of Worship

Thanks be to God, who always leads us as captives in Christ's triumphal procession and uses us to spread the aroma of the knowledge of him everywhere.

2 CORINTHIANS 2:14

In high school I had a free study hall hour that could be used for whatever I wanted. Being the overachiever that I am, I had the goal to read the Bible straight through. When I finally got to Revelation 4:6-8, it talked about angelic beings surrounding the throne and repeating the words, "Holy, holy, holy, is the Lord God Almighty, who was, and is, and is to come" (Revelation 4:8). That Scripture captivated me. The thought of those words being spoken endlessly painted a picture of how majestic our God is.

I was so struck by these words that I found myself also saying them over and over. I was mesmerized by the idea of a throne room and our God there as the mighty King, Ruler over everything, Creator of the universe, and Ruler over my own being. He is so holy and revered, that angelic beings are in complete awe of Him and repeat praise without ceasing. Amazing!

You know what else is incredible? In Zephaniah 3:17 (ESV) it says that "he will quiet you by his love; he will exult over you with loud singing." The Great I Am loves us so much that in all His glory, He sings over us! A lullaby of sorts. A song of love over His creation. Isn't that a beautiful thought?

When I was little, we had a swing that hung on an old tree outside our kitchen window. Right where my feet met the sky was a huge lilac bush. I'll never forget the intoxicating scent. That aroma is what I envision our songs of praise to be. When we sing to Him songs of thanksgiving, a scent so sweet and delicate wafts up to heaven and joins the angels as they endlessly praise.

When we praise, strongholds are literally broken off. When we worship Him, we are speaking truth, and that truth aligns our hearts for breakthrough. When we glorify Him, an inexplicable, extraordinary intimacy with our Heavenly Daddy bonds us. In its beauty and sincerity, I imagine our praise and worship has a pleasing scent that brings delight to the Lord.

The next time you feel a funk coming on, put on a praise song, destination music (I love Hawaiian music), birdsong, or whatever melody aligns your heart with Him. It will renew and ignite your heart's passion for God. A mental shift will take place and your mood will lift. Once you open your mouth and start singing words that glorify God and all that He is and does, any heaviness you're carrying will dissipate.

Before armies went into battle, they blew horns and declared advancement. What if we held our horns high? And instead of retreating in defeat when the world crashes in, we dig deep into our reservoirs of praise, line up our mouths with truth, and sing!

Think on your circumstances right now. What do you want to lift up with praise to the Lord? What past victory inspires you to sing and shout heavenward with gratitude? Have you paused to sing praises in the middle of a hardship? That is less natural to us, but in time, this habit of worshipping in all things will become our first response.

That's what David did. The Book of Psalms is filled with his story of running for his life from King Saul, hiding in caves . . . and crying out to the Lord. He used his anguish, repentance, and his revelations of God's goodness to write songs of praise. David made mistakes. He was far

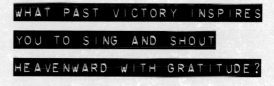

WHAT PAST VICTORY INSPIRES YOU TO SING AND SHOUT HEAVENWARD WITH GRATITUDE?

from perfect, yet he and his posture of praise were precious to the Lord. His worship was a beautiful, fragrant offering and received with love.

May this inspire your own heart of praise. We are imperfect beings, but when we sing our songs to the Lord, they become an offering. Let the aroma of your love rise to the heavens today and let it cover those you are near. Spread the knowledge of the Lord's goodness wherever you go. You will experience the sweet communion that sustains you no matter what.

You Are So Loved

Sing to the LORD a new song, his praise
from the end of the earth, you who go down
to the sea, and all that fills it,
the coastlands and their inhabitants.

ISAIAH 42:10

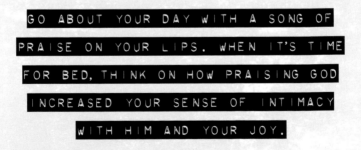

GO ABOUT YOUR DAY WITH A SONG OF
PRAISE ON YOUR LIPS. WHEN IT'S TIME
FOR BED, THINK ON HOW PRAISING GOD
INCREASED YOUR SENSE OF INTIMACY
WITH HIM AND YOUR JOY.

Lord, I'm in awe that You love me so much that You sing over me. You bless me even when I mess up. When fear tugs at my thoughts, I will think of You singing over me. The King of Kings is for me. What can possibly come against me that will matter? Who can take away the love of my Lord? No one!

When my circumstances have me feeling helpless, remind me to lift my voice and praise You. Let each offering waft to You with the scent of gratitude. The aroma of a life lived in devotion to You will give You joy. Today, I join with the scents and sounds of angels to worship You. Thank You for loving Your children so well. In Jesus's name, amen.

Change Your Focus

Do all things without grumbling or questioning, that you may be blameless and innocent, children of God without blemish in the midst of a crooked and perverse generation, among whom you shine as lights in the world, holding fast to the word of life, so that in the day of Christ I may be proud that I did not run in vain or labor in vain.

PHILIPPIANS 2:14-16 RSV

I saw a video of zinnias dancing in the breeze a while ago and it stuck with me. The view was from the ground looking up to the sky. I was amazed at how the shift in perspective changed everything. The light from the sun shining down illuminated each petal with a soft glow. The stems were the highlight instead of the blooms. Shadows wove between the flowers and their sway captivated me. I didn't want to look away from the beauty that came with the new view.

That eye-opening perspective *on* perspective got me thinking about my life and how a shift in my thoughts could change everything. I heard the phrase "blessings into burdens" recently and I was immediately drawn to repent of some mindsets I'd allowed to burrow in. I realized how I had turned some of my blessings into burdens by the way I saw them and responded to them.

The very gifts that God has given us can easily twist and become something that we take for granted, that we complain about, or worse yet . . . something we don't view as a blessing at all. Yet 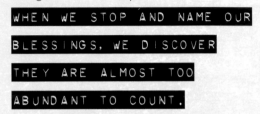 WHEN WE STOP AND NAME OUR BLESSINGS, WE DISCOVER THEY ARE ALMOST TOO ABUNDANT TO COUNT. when we stop and name our blessings, we discover they are almost too abundant to count. The air we breathe. The ability to walk and talk. The capacity to make decisions and form a thought. The gifts we've been given . . . art, cooking, writing, singing, sewing whatever it is . . . Our homes. The food on our tables. Our parents. Friends. Spouses. Children. The towns we live in. The beauty of the sunset. I could go on and on.

So why do we sometimes look on these as burdens? How do we become ungrateful?

When I think of an ungrateful heart, I think of the Israelites. They had every need miraculously met. They were delivered from slavery. They had manna and quail supernaturally appear daily, and yet they grumbled and complained. It seems impossible that we would do the same thing in that situation doesn't it? They had seen miracles with their own eyes. The Red Sea had parted, and they had been able to walk on dry ground. Surely, I wouldn't grumble or take God's provision for granted after that . . . and yet, every day I do.

Dishes in the sink. Laundry to be folded. Meals to be made. Exercise! Weeds to be pulled in my garden. The list is long for all of us. Those dishes, laundry, meals, exercise, and weeds all represent abundance. I have food. I have clothes. I have a body. I have flowers! It's my job to steward what the Lord has given me. And in my understanding, if I do so with a grateful heart, possibly singing praises to Him as I work, that praise is an offering of thanksgiving. It creates the shift in perspective that turns the mundane into marvelous. It takes the thing I dread and turns it into an act of worship.

I believe that when our heart focus goes from drudgery to praise, something wonderful is released in the heavenly realm. Maybe angels surround us and the work seems lighter? Our attitude is changed and the thing that we hated doing becomes something we no longer put off. I gladly strap on those shoes and hit the gym, because my mind remembers I'm taking care of my blessing. I no longer huff and puff at the thought of doing the dishes, because I get to care for my home and my home is a gift!

If you find yourself caught in a pattern of complaining, make the decision to change your perspective. It's not a switch you can just flip. It's going to take a major mind upheaval. It's a habit-forming, life-changing decision that not only requires focus, but also a heart postured towards repentance.

I'm ready for the challenge. I want to lay in a field and gaze upward. I want to be grateful not only for only the flowers, but for the sun, the sky, and the clouds passing by. I want fresh eyes for Him.

You Are So Loved

He humbled you, causing you to hunger and then feeding you with manna, which neither you nor your ancestors had known, to teach you that man does not live on bread alone but on every word that comes from the mouth of the Lord.

DEUTERONOMY 8:3

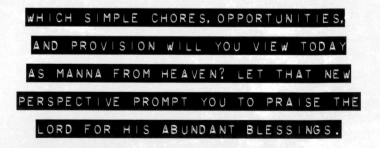

WHICH SIMPLE CHORES, OPPORTUNITIES, AND PROVISION WILL YOU VIEW TODAY AS MANNA FROM HEAVEN? LET THAT NEW PERSPECTIVE PROMPT YOU TO PRAISE THE LORD FOR HIS ABUNDANT BLESSINGS.

Lord, thank You for opening my eyes
to areas of discontent in my life.
Forgive me for taking my blessings
and turning them into burdens at
times. I ask You to convict my heart
in areas that I need to address.
Show me where I've let in an attitude
of ungratefulness, grumbling, and
complaining. Your provision is more
than enough. Your gifts are abundant.
You meet my every need, and I'm
forever grateful for everything I
have. Your Word says that every good
gift is from You. And my gifts are
too numerous to name. Thank You!

I come to You in awe and worship,
not for what Your hand provides, but
to seek Your face and to praise Your
holy name. In Jesus's name, amen.

Paint the Vision

The LORD answered me:
"Write the vision; and make it
plain on tablets."

HABAKKUK 2:2 ESV

Something special happens when you become still and you listen to what stirs your heart. How often do we do that? The busyness of ordinary life has a tendency to railroad our days, but imagine the gift of a quiet minute with just you and the Lord. What is He saying to you? What desires are buried beneath the dishes, piles of laundry, and errands?

A few years ago, I embraced this kind of moment. I asked myself what I truly wanted. And to my surprise, the answer surfaced quickly. I wanted a beautiful space to create in. That possibility wasn't even a blip on my radar at the time. We had just relocated to Tennessee from Virginia. We had poured everything into a very costly renovation. Weary from that stressful experience and tapped out financially, I hadn't let myself dream anymore because I felt like I didn't deserve it. I had everything I needed. How could I ask for or pursue more?

Then one day I took my paints out and painted the image of a simple little glasshouse on our hill. I even included the words "paint the vision" at the top. I tucked it away and didn't think about it again until I recently discovered it buried in my office. That little painting was coming true! My wildest dreams had taken flight, and an even more beautiful space was being built right where I had painted it. My heart filled with enormous gratitude. I couldn't stop thinking about the moment I first expressed my dream on the canvas and then looking out the window at the dream coming to life on our hill. My past and my present were right in front of me and God's love covered all of it. He had planted the dream and then made it come to life.

I invite you to try something right now. Take a minute to name some of your life dreams.  YOUR LIFE IS PART OF THE BIGGER STORY OF GOD'S FAITHFULNESS AND PURPOSE. Write them down. I'm not talking doable dreams. I'm talking about big God-sized dreams that could only happen if His hand was all over it. Now simply pray over those dreams in faith. Ask God for His perfect will to be done and state your case about why you want those things to come true.

God listens to our prayers and He cares about our hopes and futures. He wants us to come to Him and ask what we long to ask. Consider the truth of this verse for your life, "You do not have because you do not ask God" (James 4:2). So, let's be brave and ask our heavenly Daddy—the One who loves us more than anyone else ever could—to make some dreams come true. Do you remember a dream you had when you were younger, but you were too afraid to speak it aloud or ask God for it? It's not too late to be bold. It's never too late to ask for a dream and to then give it back to God as an offering for Him to shape into something beyond what you could imagine.

Our lives are a testimony. Your life is part of the bigger story of God's faithfulness and purpose. When good things come to pass and we share about that, we build each other's faith! Refer back to that dream list often because you will see them come to fruition and you won't be able to contain your excitement about how God is a way-maker. How He cares about all the intimate little heart desires we tuck away.

I've done this for years, and I know this is one of the reasons my faith is so strong. He hears me. He also protects me. Some of the dreams I lifted up in prayer were a really bad idea that I didn't have wisdom for at the time. And He graciously saved me from myself. Those noes are just as much of a love hug from heaven as the yeses.

Take time to be still and to pay attention to what vision emerges. Even if you can't see it clearly yet, God will help you add color and dimension. He will help you paint your vision so you can hold onto it with hope.

You Are So Loved

Still the vision awaits its appointed time;
it hastens to the end—it will not lie.
If it seems slow, wait for it; it will
surely come; it will not delay.

HABAKKUK 2:3 ESV

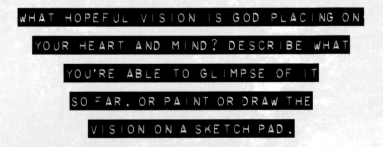

WHAT HOPEFUL VISION IS GOD PLACING ON
YOUR HEART AND MIND? DESCRIBE WHAT
YOU'RE ABLE TO GLIMPSE OF IT
SO FAR. OR PAINT OR DRAW THE
VISION ON A SKETCH PAD.

Thank You, Lord, for fulfilling Your promises to me. I awaken each day with the certainty that You love me and are making a way to impossible things. I trust You in the yeses and in the noes, and I believe that all things work together for good to those who love You.

With pen, or paint, or heart in hand, I'm going to be brave and make my requests known. Trusting what Your Word says gives me confidence to ask boldly. I know my life is a testimony of Your goodness, Your provision, and Your vision. I can't wait to see all that You have for me unfurl and to share the journey of being loved by You with others, all for Your glory. In Jesus's name, amen.

'Tis So Sweet to Trust in Jesus

You have been a refuge for the poor,
a refuge for the needy in their distress,
a shelter from the storm.

ISAIAH 25:4

A few years ago, I sat under a large tent with my family, the wind was whipping, the pastor was speaking last words over my daddy. Mom and I were huddled, holding hands, and all of a sudden the tent made a loud snap, the canvas catching in the wind. She leaned over and whispered the word "unfurled" to me. Tears immediately came, not for my daddy this time, but for the reminder of the promise the Lord had spoken over me months before. He had led me to go a different direction with my business, and in the waiting for the new, He gave me a dream of a sailboat with its sail being unfurled. I could hear a *Snap!* as it released to its full billowing size and set course for a way created and cleared by God.

"Unfurled" became my word for that year. Little did I

know that a word I had never spoken before would become a word picture that I'd refer to over and again in my mind. I had days when I felt completely aimless navigating grief. Leaning in, I desperately wanted relief from the hurt of losing my dad and clarity of next steps for a business that I knew was taking a different shape.

In time, I sensed God's presence begin to soothe the raw places. The pain started to subside. "The Spirit of God has made me; the breath of the Almighty gives me life" (Job 33:4). The same breath that gave me life was bringing me back to life. Ideas started dropping into my spirit once again, one little ripple at a time. He would give me an idea. I'd run with it as far as I could go, and then I'd wait. Never having a clue what the next steps were, I had no choice but to rest and trust that He'd give me another ripple, another little bit of forward motion when the time was right.

When I look back, I see that God navigated that whole year, and He gave me what I needed most—a respite from the frantic pace I'd been living the last several years. He carried me, pointed me in the right direction, and provided the wind I needed to get beyond the storm.

In the final moments when we took my dad off life support, my mom leaned down and sang "'Tis So Sweet to Trust in Jesus" right into his ear. His failing heart rose with her lyrics and ended with her last note. I couldn't have written a sweeter ending to his earthly life. As he passed into heaven, he was assured that trusting in Jesus was the answer. And it always is, my friend.

After my dad's passing, I leaned into God's certainty and chose another word: "tethered." I knew, especially after the way God cared for us as a family, that I wanted to be tethered to the One worth holding on to when things change, when healing is needed, when I am so depleted that I can only stand because He gives me strength. I wanted to be attached to the anchor in the storms of life. He would hold me steadfast and safe.

Just like the wind that fills a sail, the breath of God fills us and moves us toward our purpose. Pause to think about your breath right now. It rises and falls without your need to tell your body what to do. God's holy breath flows through us also. We're so blessed to be created with and carried by that breath all the days of our earthly existence. When we give ourselves over to God's strength, we are empowered by that breath, and when we are gone, His breath remains in the world. It is eternal.

Are you blowing aimlessly in the wind of your own strength or has the Lord filled your sails with purpose? Are you renewed or are you losing power? If you are off course or being tossed by the waves, call out His name. Pray for your faith journey to be tethered to Him. When you do, you will sigh a breath of relief. 'Tis so sweet to trust in Jesus.

> JUST LIKE THE WIND THAT FILLS A SAIL, THE BREATH OF GOD FILLS US AND MOVES US TOWARD OUR PURPOSE.

You Are So Loved

Lord, you are my God;
I will exalt you and praise your name,
for in perfect faithfulness
you have done wonderful things,
things planned long ago.

ISAIAH 25:1

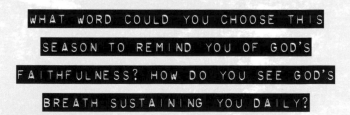

WHAT WORD COULD YOU CHOOSE THIS
SEASON TO REMIND YOU OF GOD'S
FAITHFULNESS? HOW DO YOU SEE GOD'S
BREATH SUSTAINING YOU DAILY?

Thank You, Lord, for never letting me go. Even when I feel like letting go, even when I feel like going my own way, You are holding me tightly. My life's purpose unfurled when I received Your breath. Because of Your faithfulness as Creator and Protector, I know I can trust You for all that I encounter-even grief, seasons of uncertainty, and death.

When storms arise, I am tethered to You because Your strength does not waver. Even before I call on Your name for help, You are calming the seas and winds. When I reach out, You are already there with Your eye on me. This life of mine is sweetly blessed because of the shelter of Your care. In Jesus's name, amen.

Perfect Peace

You will keep in perfect peace those whose minds are steadfast, because they trust in you.

ISAIAH 26:3

I grew up as a Midwest farm girl. We only had corn and soybean fields for as far as the eye could see surrounding our old farmhouse. Every single year, without fail, we had a plague of sorts. That sounds a little dramatic, but it was a reality on the farm. One year we had honeybees living in our walls. You could hear them humming. Then there was the year of crickets. I tried with all my might to fall asleep to their chirping . . . to no avail. Did you know they chew holes in your clothes? They do! Daddy would spray the foundation and sweep large piles of them up in our basement.

There was also the year of the fleas. And then mice. It seemed never-ending. Believe me, I've developed a keen eye for critters. I can spot a teeny tiny spider from across a room. I'm always scanning. Always searching for a pest.

I'm in my own country home now, and we've had the year of Asian beetles, carpenter bees, wasps, stink bugs, and most recently we were visited by brown recluse spiders. I wish I could unsee the spiders. I hate those creepy crawlers the most. Especially ones that could potentially harm me and my loved ones. But the fact is, nature is living large in these Tennessee hills, and it is just part of its rhythm to hatch all the things.

Nothing can steal my peace faster than a poisonous spider crawling on my couch. But I'm learning that the best way to combat the fear that pests evoke is to speak out Scriptures. For example, on any given day you'll hear me saying, "I walk in the same authority as Jesus" (Matthew 28:18), and "He has given us dominion over all the animals" (Genesis 1:26). So in the name of Jesus, these spiders, ants, stink bugs, and the others must leave!

No matter what pest or problem comes your way, you can decide whether to cower or walk in power. I choose the latter. What pests are you fighting? Is there something that evokes fear in

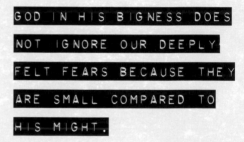

GOD IN HIS BIGNESS DOES NOT IGNORE OUR DEEPLY FELT FEARS BECAUSE THEY ARE SMALL COMPARED TO HIS MIGHT.

your heart the second you see it? Do you feel like hiding from certain circumstances instead of facing them head on? I get it, but don't camp in that place of fear and doom.

We serve a big God, and He is exceedingly able to conquer our enemies. There are times when my response to a few of God's creatures has likely made Him laugh. I've screamed and jumped in response to the sight of a snake in the lane. But God, in His bigness, does not ignore our deeply felt fears because they are small compared to His might. He doesn't turn away because we can't handle life on our own.

Instead, God sees us in our distresses (silly or severe) and remains our protector. He listens to us rant and cry. He watches us rearrange our day or our furniture to avoid encounters with something that annoys us or threatens our peace. Your pest might be a project that never ends. A coworker who intimidates you, or a problem from your past that pops its head up now and then to remind you that you haven't yet given it over to God's control.

If we become practiced at trusting Him and being steadfast in turning our fears and phobias over to Him, God will be our peace, friend. Am I going to stare down a brown recluse spider as it makes its way toward me on the couch? No! I will still run away. But no longer will I feel helpless at the sight of something that sparks fear in me. I pray you find this assurance as well, no matter what makes you afraid.

You Are So Loved

I sought the Lord, and he answered me;
he delivered me from all my fears.

PSALM 34:4

WHAT PEST OR PROBLEM DO YOU WANT TO
EXCHANGE FOR GOD'S PERFECT PEACE?

Lord, thank You for protecting me against all the things I can and cannot see. I know I can run to Your promises that keep me in perfect peace. I will stand on those promises even when I get spooked. When something evokes fear in me, calm my spirit and give me the words that steady my thoughts and nerves. You don't make me feel small for coming to You with my everyday troubles. You welcome me with open arms.

The more time I spend in Your presence, the easier it will become to go to that quiet place quickly. I will learn to draw from Your infinite peace when I face that first response of fright. Thank You for loving me so well. In Jesus's name, amen.

God with Us

"Behold, the virgin shall be with child,
and bear a Son, and they shall call His
name Immanuel," which is translated,
"God with us."

MATTHEW 1:23 NKJV

A few years ago, after my dad died, I started to notice yellow bal
loons everywhere. They appeared bouncing on shiny ribbons
and would dance in the breeze, catching my eye and reminding me of my father's joyful presence. Every celebration. Every
open house. Every store promotion . . . seemed to have yellow
balloons. Yellow became the color that tied me to my daddy.

During my walks down my country lane, I would be accom-
panied by a fluttering yellow butterfly. It became a nod, a love
hug from heaven, reminding me that my daddy was alive and
well in his new forever home.

A while back I shared my painting of a flock of cardinals
sitting in a wintery tree. Countless people wrote and told me
that the cardinal was their yellow balloon. Every time they saw a
cardinal, it triggered a memory of their loved one and they felt
an instant connection.

God makes His presence and His love known in similar

ways. He uses His creation to catch our eye and draw us to Him. We receive these gifts of connection when we notice birds, the blooms along the path, the colors of a rainbow that arch across the sky reminding us of His promises. These glimpses of meaningful images and beauty spark our hearts and make us feel seen and loved by a God who knows our every thought. Each encounter brings us closer to our Maker. These are our love hugs from our heavenly Father.

Is there anything in nature that pulls you toward the Lord? Maybe when you stand at the edge of the ocean, you realize He tells the waves where to stop. Maybe you feel His presence when you look at a mountain vista and see the expanse of His work. You notice how He formed 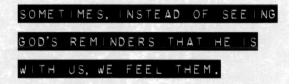 the earth into majestic peaks and valleys. Whatever it is that draws your heart to Him, it's intentional.

I have a connection with hawks. Every time I witness one soaring across the sky or perched on a telephone pole, I hear the Lord whisper to me that He's watching over me. The assurance and confidence of a regal hawk reminds me that I'm being cared for by a powerful, all-knowing Father. Each sighting is another little love hug from Him to me.

Sometimes, instead of seeing God's reminders that He is with us, we feel them. At one of his famous crusades, Billy Graham compared God to the wind. We don't see the wind, but we see and feel the effects of the wind. So it is with the mystery of God. Love hugs from God are like the wind. We might not see His arms encircle us, but we feel the embrace. The stirrings of a breeze through the trees can remind us that He's with us and knows us intimately. Each time we are reminded that we are not alone. That He is real. Close. And just a whisper away.

Scripture reminds us of God's presence in all of nature.

> By the word of the Lord the heavens were made, and by the breath of His mouth all their lights. He gathers the waters of the sea together as a heap; He puts the depths in storehouses. Let all the earth fear the Lord; Let all the inhabitants of the world stand in awe of Him. For He spoke, and it was done; He commanded, and it stood firm.
>
> PSALM 33:6–9 NASB

> The heavens declare the glory of God; the skies proclaim the work of his hands. Day after day they pour forth speech; night after night they reveal knowledge. They have no speech, they use no words; no sound is heard from them. Yet their voice goes out into all the earth, their words to the ends of the world.
>
> PSALM 19:1–4

Maybe you really need to hear this today—He is with you. His presence is alive. And if you've invited Him into your life, He lives in your heart. When you need reminders of His all-encompassing love; pause and listen, and you'll feel the evidence of His presence and receive His love hugs.

You Are So Loved

Where can I go from your Spirit? Where can I flee from your presence? . . . If I rise on the wings of the dawn, if I settle on the far side of the sea, even there your hand will guide me, your right hand will hold me fast.

PSALM 139:7-10

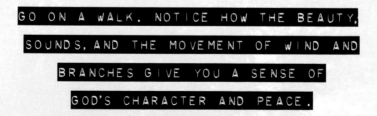
GO ON A WALK. NOTICE HOW THE BEAUTY, SOUNDS, AND THE MOVEMENT OF WIND AND BRANCHES GIVE YOU A SENSE OF GOD'S CHARACTER AND PEACE.

God, open my eyes to see You in everything. You are right here in the beauty that surrounds me. I see You in the mountains, valleys, oceans, and trees. I rejoice because You can use anything from balloons to birds to draw me close. May the images that speak to my spirit also quicken my heart to the need for a Savior.

Thank You for sending Jesus to be among us. He appeared in flesh and blood. His feet walked this earth and His hands touched and healed many. I thank You today that because of the finished work of the cross, He lives inside me and is closer than ever! Jesus was and is the ultimate love hug from heaven. I am forever grateful. In Jesus's name, amen!

Safe Place

"He must become greater; I must become less." The one who comes from above is above all.

JOHN 3:30-31

My dad was my earthly sense of God's comfort and safety. The peace that flooded my heart when we'd talk about my worries was palpable. He never got flustered. He just listened and said it would all work out. And he was always right. Throughout my life, my dad's faith steadied my emotions and increased my own faith.

After he passed away, I clung to God with an even greater love and dependence. I knew He was my protector and the one who would speak words of comfort over me whenever the waves of grief came and life was difficult. When the first holiday season approached after my dad's death, I knew I was headed for an emotionally tough time, so we booked a trip to our family's happy place . . . Hawaii. I was seeking respite from my grief. Chasing rainbows, so to speak. I needed the numb to be replaced with joy.

There I was on Christmas Day, standing at the edge of the ocean. My feet were buried in the sand; I was mesmerized by the waves. The bronze glitter beneath me swirled and churned, and as each wave receded, my foundation eroded. Wave after wave, my body sank a little deeper. Each minuscule grain was carried off and then replaced with the next swell. After what felt like the longest pause I'd had in years, I started to cry. Not

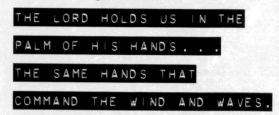

THE LORD HOLDS US IN THE PALM OF HIS HANDS . . . THE SAME HANDS THAT COMMAND THE WIND AND WAVES.

from sadness, but from revelation. With each ebb and flow of the sea waters, I heard in my mind, *More of You, less of me*. That's what the Lord was telling me. Waves crashing, the mantra repeated, *More of Him . . . less of me!* over and over.

The "download" began. My mind filled with truths of who He is. He is my portion. My foundation. My safe place. My focus. My reason to breathe. The filler of my soul. The righter of all wrongs. He's mysterious, majestic, and able to do abundantly more than I could ever imagine.

My tears turned into a silent plea that mimicked the current, "Empty me. Fill me. Empty me. Fill me . . . with You!" In a way, that day at the beach was a nudge. My heavenly Daddy was reminding me that my sense of well-being doesn't rely on positive affirmation and earthly relationships. It relies on my dependence in Him.

Isn't it amazing to think that He controls the wind and waves?

> *Suddenly a furious storm came up on the lake, so that the waves swept over the boat. But Jesus was sleeping. The disciples went and woke him, saying, "Lord, save us! We're going to drown!" He replied, "You of little faith, why are you so afraid?" Then he got up and rebuked the winds and the waves, and it was completely calm. The men were amazed and asked, "What kind of man is this? Even the winds and the waves obey him!"*
>
> MATTHEW 8:24–27

> *Then Moses stretched out his hand over the sea, and all that night the Lord drove the sea back with a strong east wind and turned it into dry land. The waters were divided, and the Israelites went through the sea on dry ground, with a wall of water on their right and on their left.*
>
> EXODUS 14:21–22

He held back the Red Sea for the Israelites so they could escape slavery. He does that for us too. He makes a path for us and leads us to safety. God creates the way through our difficulties so we don't ever question that He's the One who protects us and is the One we can run to. His presence is our ultimate escape. When we create a daily practice of surrendering our needs to Him, we can face the path and the unknowns with confidence. The Lord holds us in the palm of His hands . . . the same hands that command the wind and waves.

Oh, how this is the reassurance that I need to let it all go. I pray it's the truth that allows you to release your fears and any other reasons you hesitate giving everything to the Lord. May His presence and peace increase in your life in amazing ways.

You Are So Loved

God is my strength and power,
And He makes my way perfect.

2 SAMUEL 22:33 NKJV

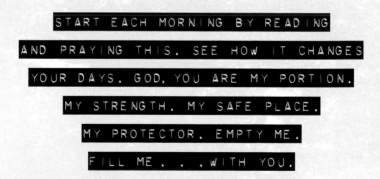

START EACH MORNING BY READING
AND PRAYING THIS. SEE HOW IT CHANGES
YOUR DAYS. GOD, YOU ARE MY PORTION.
MY STRENGTH. MY SAFE PLACE.
MY PROTECTOR. EMPTY ME.
FILL ME. . . .WITH YOU.

Lord, I'm thankful that You are
so full of power and might that I
can rest in Your greatness. In my
human frailty, I can lean into Your
strength and surrender. Thank You
that You give me comfort and peace
when everything else leaves me
feeling hollow. When I feel alone or
lose my earthly safety nets, I have
no need to be afraid. I will always
have You by my side . . . and
going before me!

You usher me into new seasons and,
through Your faithfulness, remind me
of Your sovereignty. My plea to be
emptied and filled by You is met by
Your mercies. I love You, Lord. In
this life, I will forever need less
of me and more of You. Always You.
In Jesus's name. Amen.

The Gift of Blessing

**All peoples on earth will be
blessed through you.**

GENESIS 12:3

My earliest memories of my mama are of hearing her pray. She made a tiny prayer closet in the bottom of the attic stairwell next to my bedroom. This small space had a miniature wooden table where she kept her Bible and prayer journal. The tattered wallpapered walls were covered with pictures of our family and friends. Through the plaster I could hear her pleading with God about matters that were on her heart.

She wept and sang and petitioned the Lord for a good part of every morning. She set the precedent for me to know what a godly woman looked like. She was flawed, but her genuine love for the Lord and willingness to share Him with everyone she met was unparalleled.

When I first got married, she came over to our tiny apartment with a friend. Full of faith and revelation after a Christian conference they had just attended, she gave me the greatest gift

I've ever received. She cradled my face in her hands and spoke a blessing over my life.

It wasn't the first time I received a blessing, but it's the one I'll never forget. It was moving, beautiful. She spoke to my giftings, she spoke to our financial future, she spoke to my mental health and declared that I would be so full of joy that my lips would never stop singing His praises. It was powerful, and to this day I can remember that moment in time like it was yesterday.

Those words of blessing have come true. Our lives have had tremendous favor. I have seen the Lord carry us through multiple moves, through tremendous attacks from the enemy, through mountaintop experiences and low valleys. His hand has always been present and I've felt His presence close. And despite some of the valleys, my faith didn't waver because I knew He was the giver of every good gift in my life.

Did you know as sons and daughters of God we all possess this amazing gift of blessing? We can do this daily. The Bible mentions blessing many times, but I particularly love this passage.

> *The Lord your God will bless you in the land he is giving you. The Lord will establish you as his holy people, as he promised you on oath, if you keep the commands of the Lord your God and walk in obedience to him . . . The Lord will open the heavens, the storehouse of his bounty, to send rain on your land in season and to bless all the work of your hands.*
>
> DEUTERONOMY 28:8-9,12

A blessing is a life-changing experience. Speaking truth over someone with your words and identifying the good you see in them—the talents, abilities, giftings, and unique qualities they may be unaware of—is life-giving. It lines them up with their purpose and reveals to them the ways they bless others.

Our words, whether a blessing or a curse, are seeds that carry weight and take root. This also applies to what we say to  ourselves. How many times a day do you think or speak a negative thought about yourself? I'm the queen of self-deprecation. I often point out my flaws before other people notice them, just so they know that I know I'm not perfect. Let's choose to speak positively about ourselves. Line yourself up with what God says over us and confess those things instead!

Let's make it our mission to use our words as a gift of blessing! So, who can you bless today? Does your mother, sister, child, husband, boss, or friend need to hear something that will encourage them forever? I bet they do! Maybe you grew up with curses instead of blessing? I'm praying for your heart right now. Ask the Lord to bring to mind someone close to you, who knows you well, and ask them to speak a blessing into your life. It's okay to ask. Receive those words for what they are . . . truth from heaven.

So how do you impart a blessing? Ask the Lord to fill your mouth with words regarding the person's life. Ask Him to open your eyes to their strengths . . . to see them as He does. Then ask the Holy Spirit to give you the boldness to speak into their lives. He always will.

You Are So Loved

There, in the presence of the LORD your God,
you and your families shall eat and shall
rejoice in everything you have put your hand
to, because the LORD your God has blessed you.

DEUTERONOMY 12:7

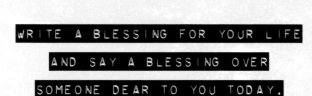

WRITE A BLESSING FOR YOUR LIFE
AND SAY A BLESSING OVER
SOMEONE DEAR TO YOU TODAY.

Lord, thank You for blessing Your people countless times throughout history and continuing to do so today. I love the blessing You spoke over Abraham in Genesis 12. He was a faithful man, full of righteousness, and You used Him mightily to bless many nations. Thank You that, because of my faith, I'm a child of Abraham and I too share in that blessing.

Lord, bring to my mind someone I can extend blessing to today. I want to change lives with life-giving words . . . Your words. You have abundantly blessed my life. I will walk in those blessings and my lips will forever sing Your praises because You are good, faithful, and You fill my heart with gladness. I love You so much, Lord! In Jesus's name, amen.

Listen for His Voice

My sheep listen to my voice;
I know them, and they follow me.

JOHN 10:27

The view from our hill looks across the valley to another farm. On most days the hill in front of that house is scattered with sheep. With their heads down, they look like little white stat ues. I spent some time looking into more information about their nature and found a video of people calling out to sheep. Three different "testers" were trying to get the sheep's attention. The sheep ignored each one, munching on the grass in front of them, completely oblivious to the callers.

Then the farmer—their owner—stepped up and shouted out his call.

One by one, each head popped up, and without hesitation they started running to his voice. I watched that video with tears streaming down my face. I immediately thought of John 10:27. When our Shepherd is the Lord, we are in tune with Him. We know Him, He knows us, and nothing can sway our attention. We run to His voice and listen.

As Shepherd, God is our Protector, Companion, and the Guide to lead us safely along the path of life. When we spend time with Him, read His Word, and recognize our dependence on Him for all this, we raise our heads and listen. Our response is *always* to follow. And His response is to always provide.

Have you had times when hearing the Shepherd's voice was more difficult? There are seasons when we feel distant or our circumstances, other people's expectations, or the chaos of the world distracts us. It drowns out the voice that will lead us safely along our path and safely home.

Learning to be still and to hear God can be a daily practice. When I think of Him as 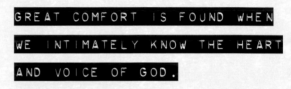 Shepherd, I imagine going about my day and looking up to see His reassuring presence in the field with me. He is looking out for danger, He is watching the path ahead to make sure I am heading the right way, and He calls my name not only to be sure I am still with Him, but to remind me of His love.

Great comfort is found when we intimately know the heart and voice of God. We don't have to question or be fearful. There are ways to become a sheep who clearly hears the voice of the Shepherd.

Believe He's the Good Shepherd. Do you believe He is among His sheep to save you? Love you? Guide you along the craggy hills, the rolling fields, and the steep mountain sides? Friend, when you spend any time in the presence of the Shepherd, you will know this is true!

Place His Word on your heart. Spend time in God's Word daily so you know the truth and tone of the Father's voice. Reading His love letter to you again and again will make your heart tender toward

His message and your ears in tune with His voice . . . even when life gets crazy, loud, and busy.

Talk to Him. Prayer is simply a conversation. Talking and listening. Just like any friendship, the more you talk to your friend and listen, the deeper the connection.

Ask for discernment and wisdom. We all need this! As smart as we may become in the work He gives us to do, we will only remain on the right path if we're discerning. "If any of you lacks wisdom, you should ask God, who gives generously to all without finding fault, and it will be given to you" (James 1:5). We only need to ask. Don't be shy. I ask all the time because I never want to assume I know the big picture or whether to go left or right without the Shepherd's guidance.

I once had a dream that a herd of sheep were charging up our hill with great determination. When I awoke, I immediately knew that was spiritual—a vision of revival. I will be a part of that herd running toward God's voice, His heart, and His glory. Lean into the Master Shepherd and hear His voice. Let's run together with purpose and follow our Shepherd's call.

You Are So Loved

The LORD is my shepherd, I lack nothing.
He makes me lie down in green pastures,
he leads me beside quiet waters,
he refreshes my soul.

PSALM 23:1-3

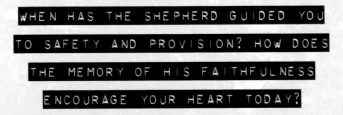

WHEN HAS THE SHEPHERD GUIDED YOU
TO SAFETY AND PROVISION? HOW DOES
THE MEMORY OF HIS FAITHFULNESS
ENCOURAGE YOUR HEART TODAY?

Lord, thank You for loving me so much
that You sacrificed greatly to be
my Shepherd. You call my name and I
respond because I know Your voice.
Even when You tell me to move into
the unknown, I trust You're with me.
When You say danger is near, I will
draw closer to Your safe presence
without hesitation.

Lord, open my ears so I know the
difference between Your voice and
the voices of those who want to
harm me or lead me astray. I ask for
Your wisdom and discernment daily.
Protect my heart so it doesn't become
hardened and is always ready to
hear You call my name with love. I
want for nothing because You are my
faithful Shepherd.

Walk Worthy

Be filled with the knowledge of His will
in all wisdom and spiritual understanding;
that you may walk worthy of the Lord.

COLOSSIANS 1:9-10 NKJV

The word "holiness" is a bit intimidating, isn't it? It makes me feel small, and like I could never in a million years measure up to that standard. But when I think of God being holy, it's different. He's God! Of course, He's set apart. Flawless. But did you know that when you become part of His family you are holy too? It's mind-blowing, but it says in Leviticus 11:45 (KJV), "I am the LORD that bringeth you up out of the land of Egypt, to be your God: ye shall therefore be holy, for I am holy." Because He's holy, so are we.

When Moses went up on Mount Sinai to ponder the future of the Israelites and to get alone with God, he encountered a burning bush that was miraculously not consumed by the fire. Through that, God said, "Take off your sandals, for the place where you are standing is holy ground" (Exodus 3:5). In our human understanding, we think shoes might have been a good idea. But the shoes were a manmade separation between Moses and God's holiness. Shoes were removed by priests entering holy places, and in Jewish culture they are removed when entering a home. Moses's bare feet being on holy ground was a sign of respect, submission, and surrender, declaring God as his home. Isn't that a beautiful thought? God as home!

We can never achieve holiness on our own. Jesus's sacrifice on the cross covered our sin and made us worthy to stand before God. When the Lord looks at you, He sees His child, blameless and pure. He's pleased with you. He loves you with the greatest love imaginable. Do you struggle with feeling good enough to be loved by the Lord?

It's easy to get caught up in the trap of working for

your salvation and His approval. *If I do this. If I behave this way. If I serve. If I read. If I pray. If I give.* These are all good ideas that come from a servant heart, but in Ephesians 2:8-9 (NKJV) Paul wrote, "By grace you have been saved through faith, and that not of yourselves; it is the gift of God, not of works, lest anyone should boast." I love that verse. It removes the pressure to work for the love of Christ. He's taken care of that. We can't diminish His sacrifice by trying to add to what's already been done. Because of that enormous gift, our lives are changed. Our walk is changed.

We, being made new, naturally walk differently. Upright. Set apart. Noticeably different from the world. Paul wrote a letter to the Christians at Colossae and in verse 10 he wrote, "that you may *walk worthy* of the Lord, fully pleasing Him, being fruitful in every good work and increasing in the knowledge of the God" (Colossians 1:10 NKJV). Walk worthy—those words jumped out at me when

I read that verse.

Even today, merely typing those words makes me tear up. Oh, that my life would be worthy. This isn't a condemning verse. It's a verse that brings our hearts into alignment and makes our gaze a little higher. It reminds me of my purpose while on this earth. It's to walk worthy of the sacrifice that was given. To lay down my selfish ways and remember that He died for me. That my life would be worthy of that gift. Glory!

I love old churches with stained glass windows that let light cascade into the sanctuary as beautiful, biblical scenes, saturated in color, depict the most powerful story of all time. It feels holy, doesn't it? The light pouring in draws our eyes to the workmanship and wonder of each panel. Imagine your life fashioned into a series of those panes. Your "God story" for all to see. I wonder what mine would look like? What would yours look like? Would it be a life of walking worthy . . . a life hopelessly devoted to the One who gave it all?

You Are So Loved

If by grace, then it cannot be
based on works; if it were, grace
would no longer be grace.

ROMANS II:6

SURRENDER YOUR STRIVING
THIS WEEK. WALK WORTHY AND
LEAN INTO THE GRACE OF GOD.

Lord, You are my home. Your presence
is my safe place. I'm grateful that
I can come to You about anything.
You hear me. You see me. I am Yours.
Your instructions for me through the
words of Paul support my path. I
pray such wisdom will take root so
my life will be a living sacrifice
to You. I know I don't have to earn
my way, You already paid that price.

I want my life to matter. Guide my
steps so I walk worthy of You and
the fruit of my work is pleasing
to You. It is my joy, Lord, to make
an offering of my days, thoughts,
actions, and dreams to serve and
love You with a heart of gratitude.
In Jesus's name, amen.

ACKNOWLEDGMENTS

I've read acknowledgment pages in books for years and until now I had no idea how heart-wrenchingly important those words were for the author. Saying thank you is everything, so let me start by thanking my precious Jesus for His sacrifice on the cross. He gave me this life of freedom and the ability to see His hand in everything. Because of Him I can express myself in written word and through painting. I'll never take for granted the gifts of creativity He's given.

Thank you to my loves—Brian, Maggie, and Felicity—for putting up with me over the last year and not letting me quit. You are my forever cheerleaders, my faithful editors, and my greatest love hugs from heaven. I'm so glad you're on my side.

To my Mama Dixie, the one who introduced me to Jesus all those years ago at our kitchen table and who sees me and prays with fervor over my life. I'm forever grateful.

To Ruth, who went to bat to make this book happen.

To Hope, who took my ramblings and polished them up pretty.

To Harvest House for taking a chance on me.

To Meg, Tara, and Honey, who spoke words of encouragement and truth to make me go for it.

To Melissa, for reminding me Who holds my paintbrush.

And finally, to my precious Farmgirl Paints family. You've walked through a decade of life with me and spoken this book into existence more times than I can count. Thank you for following along, for encouraging my faith walk, and for giving me someone to share with. This book is because of you.

ABOUT BECKY

Becky Strahle is the owner of Farmgirl Paints and has been sharing her creativity and faith by designing custom hand-stamped jewelry for more than a decade, and through her recent endeavors—a love letter subscription and a jewelry box. She is a self-taught artist, and her painting medium is acrylic. Her heart's desire is to always point to Jesus, the lover of our souls.

Becky has been married to her high school sweetheart, Brian, for 29 years, and together they have two creative daughters, Maggie and Felicity. They live in the hills of Tennessee.

To connect and learn more about
Becky, visit her here:

Instagram @farmgirlpaints

www.farmgirlpaints.com

Cover and interior design by Jay and Kristi Smith–Juicebox Designs
Photos on pages 2, 8, 10 (bottom), 13, and 112-113 by Tisha Lynn
Photos on pages 4, 7, 10 (top), and 57 by Becky Strahle
Photo on page 56 by Leslie Brown
Photo on 175 by Leslie Brown Photography, courtesy of *Eden & Vine* magazine

M̄ This logo is a federally registered trademark of the Hawkins Children's LLC. Harvest House Publishers, Inc., is the exclusive licensee of this trademark.

Seeing God in the Sweet Ordinary
Text and artwork copyright © 2022 by Becky Strahle
Published by Harvest House Publishers
Eugene, Oregon 97408
www.harvesthousepublishers.com

ISBN 978-0-7369-8536-9 (hardcover)
ISBN 978-0-7369-8537-6 (eBook)

Library of Congress Control Number: 2022931415

Printed in China

22 23 24 25 26 27 28 29 30 / RDS√ 10 9 8 7 6 5 4 3 2 1